MANAGING THE IMPACT OF THE EURO

Managing the Impact of the Euro

Simon Sear

Gower

© S Sear 1998

332.494

843 m

Published by
Gower Publishing Limited
Gower House
Croft Road
Aldershot
Hampshire GU11 3HR
England

Gower
Old Post Road
Brookfield
Vermont 05036
USA

British Library Cataloguing in Publication Data
Sear, Simon

JK   Managing the impact of the Euro
     1. Monetary unions – Europe 2. Currency question – Europe
     I. Title
     332.4'5

ISBN 0 566 08146 6

Printed in Great Britain at the University Press, Cambridge

Contents

Introduction

On 27th October 1997 the British government announced that, in principle, it intends to join economic and monetary union (EMU) when the economic climate is correct, although this is not likely to be before the next election, around 2001–2002. The temptation for UK businesses is to think that they do not have to do anything about EMU because it is likely to be at least four years before we join, even if the people can be convinced of its virtues via a referendum. This, however, is a misconception; EMU will affect UK businesses from 1st January 1999, even though we are not directly participating in EMU.

The introduction of EMU will transcend every aspect of European business. In fact, it will have an impact on every country in the world that trades with countries that implement EMU during the first wave. In particular, it will have a large impact on the world's financial markets and everyone involved with them. Since around 60per cent of the UK's export trade is with other European countries joining EMU and the City of London is a world-leading financial market, that means us.

There will be effects on all UK companies

Major corporations, such as Mercedes Benz, BMW and Siemens, are already committed to using Euros at the earliest opportunity. Mercedes

Benz, for example, intend to use Euros from day one, 1ˢᵗ January 1999: they will pay their employees in Euros, pay their suppliers in Euros, quote their prices in Euros and have their capital share value converted to Euros. This will mean that anyone they come into contact with will have to have the ability to trade in the Euro. Dealerships in the UK will have to convert prices from Euros to sterling and back again. Suppliers must make demands for payment in Euros and will be paid in Euros, and in turn, their banks will have to cope with this form of payment.

The impact is enormous and the risks to a business of not finding out what exactly the effects will be, for example the implications on working practices, operations and IT systems, are substantial enough to undermine a business's ability to carry out its normal activities. For some companies, who are not prepared, EMU will mean *business disadvantage*.

It will not just be a case of dual currencies, but will involve a more complex solution. How will suppliers want to be paid? How will customers pay you? Can your accounts systems cope? What will be the affect on long-term contracts? How will it affect your tax position? The list is vast. *In fact, it is so vast it will have a higher cost implication and require greater effort than the Millennium issue.*

Financial organisations must be ready on 1ˢᵗ January 1999

Monetary union will have a huge effect on all financial organisations within the UK from 1ˢᵗ January 1999, even though the UK is not committed to joining at that time. The main consequence of EMU will be the formulation of the single currency and there will be implications across the financial sector.

All countries that join must operate their equity markets in Euros. The European stock markets have already agreed on a big bang approach to operating in the Euro from 4ᵗʰ January 1999. This means that quotations displayed on traders' screens will be in Euros and transactions will be executed, recorded, matched, confirmed and passed to settlement in Euros. The implications of the single currency on European equities will be worldwide and organisations based in the UK must consider them as part of a business impact assessment.

The EU believes that the early redenomination of sovereign debt is desirable, but not essential, for the transition from the use of national currencies to the use of the Euro. This will have consequences for anyone operating in the European bond market. New issues will also be in Euros from January 1999, and even sooner for some derivative-based products. As a result, individuals', fund managers' and governments' debt portfolios will change overnight. Coping with the physical changes and reviewing the likely strategic impact on the European bond market must be an early consideration.

The Wholesale Payment Systems are also set to change as a result of EMU. Major changes are planned, such as the introduction of the Trans-European Automated Real-Time Gross Settlement Express Transfer System (TARGET). There will also be effects on Euroclear, SWIFT, CHAPS and European Real-Time Gross Settlement Systems.

Ultimately, all UK companies, especially financial, will be affected by the introduction of EMU. In order to avoid any business disadvantage and gain business advantage they must carry out a thorough business impact assessment on the implications of EMU. This should include an assessment of the risks an organisation faces, the development of a strategic approach to managing the issue and then the implementation of a project of change to realise successful business and technical solutions.

This book is a comprehensive and practical guide for those undertaking a project to deal with the introduction of the Euro on 1st January 1999. Chapter 1 outlines what EMU is and then describes the implications for UK businesses, including illustrations of major corporate strategies, such as those of Marks and Spencer and Barclays Bank. This information provides readers with the ability to make informed decisions about their own company's strategic approach to EMU.

Chapter 2 presents the specific business implications for financial organisations. It presents detailed information for front and back office business areas, including changes in the structure of the European equity markets, the UK equity market, the European bond market, derivatives, settlement systems, and so on. Detailed information identifies the risks and issues companies face and specific implications for business processes that must be addressed.

Chapter 3 focuses on the implications for supporting IT systems. Full details of system impacts such as the use of two decimal places in nominal values and the use of six significant figures in the conversion of currencies are presented.

In Chapter 4 a review of the main information service providers is undertaken: Bridge, Bloomberg, Reuters, ICV/Datastream and FTI. Since many organisations rely heavily on the information they receive from such sources the importance of understanding their approach is crucial.

Managing the introduction of the Euro will be critical, especially since it will be upon us in January 1999. After the previous chapters assessing the impacts Chapter 5 focuses on developing both business and IT solutions to reduce the risks and resolve the issues identified. It covers design and development, testing and implementation, including the conversion weekend.

Chapter 6 covers the infrastructure required to manage a Euro programme. This includes the roles and responsibilities of a steering committee, programme manager, expert consultants, business analysts and users.

Buying new IT systems will require analysis of their Euro compliance for now and in the future when the UK joins. The Millennium Timebomb has illustrated the problems of not thinking ahead. In Chapter 7 an outline for the compliance of new products both now and in the event that the UK joins is put forward. It is hoped that this will help readers develop their own Euro compliance strategy and appropriate documentation. Even if you find you are not directly affected by the introduction of the Euro in 1999, having a Euro compliance strategy could save you substantial costs in the longer term.

Finally, a list of information sources is presented. This is a list of publications used in the creation of this book and essential Website addresses, such as those of the Bank of England, the European Union and HM Treasury.

A final note

Managing the effects of EMU on any business is not about being for or against it, pro-EMU or anti-EMU it is about avoiding *business disadvantage* that will result from companies being ill-prepared, and, perhaps, actually gaining *business advantage* through opportunities in the market. This book is written from a neutral stance and only aims to present unbiased information. It is not a political tool, but a business one.

1   Background to EMU

Economic and monetary union is a three-stage process of integration within the European Union. Stage 1 essentially concerned the fiscal and monetary co-operation of member states and was completed between July 1990 and December 1993. Stage 2 started in January 1995 and is due to complete in December 1998. This phase addresses budgets and economic aspects of the member states and the administration and implementation of monetary union in stage 3, due to take place between January 1999 and July 2002.

The third stage was agreed to begin on 1st January 1999 by European leaders in Madrid in December 1995. On this date it is intended that at least some of the member countries will have their currencies locked together at irrevocably fixed exchange rates and that the Euro be introduced as the common currency which will fully replace participating national currencies by July 2002 at the latest.

This is the final stage of economic and monetary union and will have the most substantial impact on UK businesses. Understanding the implications of stage 3 is the key to businesses effectively managing its introduction. Since it is to begin in January 1999 organisations must prepare for it now, even though the UK government has not immediately opted in.

Stage 3 – Obligations of monetary union

The Madrid summit outlined the steps that need to be taken to achieve European economic and monetary union before July 2002. The following table is a summary of this timetable:

❑ **Phase A: First half of 1998**	European Commission and European Monetary Institute (EMI) to report on convergence to the Economic and Finance Committee (ECOFIN).
	ECOFIN to assess which member states qualify for monetary union.
May 1998	Those countries intending to join are announced.
May 1998	Foreign exchange rates are announced for national legacy currencies and the Euro.
❑ **Phase A: Second half of 1998**	ECOFIN adopts secondary legislation governing European Central Bank (ECB) powers, capital and foreign exchange reserves.
	European Central Bank Executive Board appointed by heads of state/government; European System of Central Banks (ESCB) and European Central Bank to be established.
	ECB Governing Council adopts regulatory, organisational and logistical framework and tests systems in preparation for full operation in stage 3.
	A date is set for the introduction of Euro notes and coinage; physical preparations for production begin.
	ECOFIN decides the basis for selecting conversion rates to be adopted on 1st January 1999.
❑ **Phase B: 1st January 1999**	Stage 3 starts.
	ECOFIN adopts irrevocably fixed conversion rates for participating currencies and the Euro.
	Council Regulation on the legal status of the Euro enters into force.
	Euro, as a currency in its own right, replaces the ECU at a rate of 1:1.
	'Legally enforceable equivalence' between national currencies and the Euro.

		ESCB's money market and foreign exchange operations are conducted only in Euros.
		Trans-European Automated Real-Time Gross Settlement Express Transfer System (TARGET) for cross-border payments in Euros becomes operational.
		New issues of public debt of participants are in Euros only.
		'No compulsion, no prohibition' on private sector use of the Euro. During this period organisations have the option to transfer to operating in the Euro.
		National currency banknotes may be exchange at central banks at par.
❑	**Phase C: 1ˢᵗ January 2002 – 1ˢᵗ July 2002**	Euro notes and coins are introduced, with legal tender status; national currency notes and coins are withdrawn.
		Private sector companies must be operating in the Euro.
		Changeover of public sector operations to the Euro is completed.
❑	**Phase C: 2002 (at the latest)**	Any outstanding public debt still denominated in national currency is redeemable only in Euros.
		National currency notes and coins cease to be legal tender.

The table shows that the third stage of monetary union will be delivered in three distinct phases. These can be described further.

Phase A: 1998

During the first half of 1998 a decision must be made as to which countries will participate in the locking of currencies in 1999 and which countries will be allowed to proceed with a delayed version of European economic and monetary union. However, member states must join unless they fail to meet the relevant criteria. This is with the exception of the UK, who have so far negotiated a neutral position, to be able to decide when the time comes as to whether or not the UK would participate in monetary union, if it meets the convergence criteria. Currently it is widely accepted that 11 of the 15 EU members will join EMU at this stage. Only Denmark, Sweden, Greece and the UK are likely to opt out or miss the convergence criteria.

What are the convergence criteria?

At the end of the first quarter in 1998 the European Commission (EC) and the European Monetary Institute (EMI) will present two reports to the Economic and Finance Committee (ECOFIN). These reports will contain information on each member country's economic performance. Particular reference will be made to *convergence criteria*. These include:

Price stability

The rate of inflation for any one country should not exceed 1.5 per cent above that of the average.

Sustainable government financial position

The ratio of general annual deficit to GDP should not be greater than 3 per cent, unless it has declined substantially and continually and is close to the 3 per cent level. Also, the ratios of stock of government debt should not be greater than 60 per cent.

Convergence of interest rates

The long-term interest rate over the last year should not exceed the average by 2 per cent.

Exchange rate stability

Member countries should participate in the Exchange Rate Mechanism, 'respecting the normal margins of fluctuations'.

The results of the ECOFIN meeting will contain a list of those countries that have met the convergence criteria and confirm those entering into stage 3 of monetary union in January 1999. This report is scheduled for the first week in May. At this time exchange rates between the joining members and the Euro will be formulated. Since the Euro will replace the ECU 1:1 in January 1999 these exchange rates are likely to reflect existing ECU : national currency FX (financial exchange) rates.

Establishment of the European Central Bank

Once the participants have been agreed the European Central Bank (ECB) will replace the European Monetary Institute (EMI). This will continue to set the framework and systems necessary for the implementation of monetary policy on 1ˢᵗ January 1999. It will be directed by a governing board, made up of governors from participating countries' central banks and an executive board appointed from the defunct EMI.

It will be independent of individual national governments and EU institutions and fundamental changes in its statute would require the unanimous agreement of all member states.

The Maastricht Treaty requires the adoption of fixed conversion rates. This will be one of the first major roles of the Central Bank. They will be responsible for finalising how conversion rates are calculated when the Euro is introduced.

Phase B: Stage 3 starts

On 1ˢᵗ January 1999 all participating member state currencies will be locked together at irrevocably fixed conversion rates. At the same time, the Euro will be launched as a currency in its own right, but only in a scriptural format. This means that participating national currencies will have 'legally enforceable equivalence'. Member state national currencies will then be interchangeable with the Euro.

From the start of this phase the Central Bank will, in conjunction with participating member states' banks, also set the EU monetary policy. This will be achieved through money market operations using Euros and involve only non-EU currencies. A new Trans-European Automated Real-Time Gross Settlement Express Transfer System (TARGET) for the cross-border payments will be set up to enable this to happen.

From January 1999 through to July 2002 (see chapter 2 on bond markets) all new issues of government bonds will be in Euros and participating governments will have the opportunity to convert their existing debt. In addition, private organisations will be allowed to freely use the Euro during this phase, but are not obliged to. This period will allow for a bedding down of the Euro. It is intended to provide an opportunity for it to become established in the wholesale financial markets before its wider introduction across all sectors of the economy.

In the latter half of this period national banknotes will be phased out and Euros will be phased in at the exchange rates set during the beginning of this phase. The phasing in of the Euro coinage will be dependent on the demands of the member states. Some will be ready sooner than others and it may be that the benefits obtainable through introducing physical money will encourage members to introduce it at the earliest opportunity, i.e. before January 2002.

Legal aspects

The introduction of the Euro in January 1999 is backed up by legislation from the European Commission, presented in Regulation 235. This limited amount of legislation provides a framework for the use of the Euro. It can be summarised as:

Article 3

- All references to ECU will be understood to mean Euro.
- EMU cannot be used as a reason for the breaking or changing of a contract.
- Translation of currencies must follow the conversion rules, re rounding effects (see Articles 4 and 5).

Article 4

- When currencies are irrevocably fixed they shall be adopted with six significant figures.
- The conversion rates shall not be rounded or truncated when conversions are being made.
- The conversion rates shall be used for conversion either way. Inverse rates derived from conversion rates shall not be used. This is because inverse rates would produce inaccurate results for large sums.
- Monetary amounts to be converted from one national currency to another will first be converted into the Euro. This amount shall not be rounded less than three decimal places. **No alternative method of calculation may be used unless it produces the same result.**

It is not necessary to record the results of these steps. As long as the final result is correct that is the information that must be held.

Article 5

- When rounding takes place, due to a conversion into the Euro, it shall be to the nearest cent.
- When rounding takes place within a national currency it shall be to the nearest sub-unit or unit or, according to national law, the nearest multiple or fraction of a sub-unit.
- If a conversion produces a rate that is exactly half way, the sum shall be rounded up.

The rounding procedures apply to all EU member countries. This means that even though the UK will not join in the first wave of monetary union, in 1999, it will have to use the rounding and conversion principles in any currency transactions.

Article 8

Any amount denominated either in the Euro unit or in the national currency of a participating member, and payable within that state by crediting an account of the creditor, can be paid by the debtor in the Euro or the national currency unit (subject to any specific agreements made between organisations).

For the UK, it means there will be no fixed relationship between the Euro and the pound. Usual foreign exchange market conventions will apply. It is not known at this time whether the British government will place the pound within a mechanism, like the ERM, which, although not irrevocably fixed, tracks the Euro within agreed pegs.

In addition to these articles from Regulation 235, the European Commission has also introduced an ISO-approved currency symbol and hopes to gain approval for its new symbol early in 1998.

'EUR' – The new currency code for the Euro

On 21st April 1997 the maintenance agency of the International Organisation for Standardisation (ISO 4217) attributed the code 'EUR' for the Euro. This will be the international standard for any organisation, retail, commercial or financial.

The use of the Euro symbol

Since the European Council meeting in Dublin on 13th and 14th December 1996, the Commission is using the € symbol. The Commission invites the wide-scale use of this symbol by business and commerce and has applied to the International Organisation for Standardisation (ISO) for standardisation of glyphs and fonts, keyboards, character transactions, and so on.

Phase C: Full introduction of the Euro currency

During the first half of 2002 the last remaining national currencies will be removed from the participating members' economies and replaced with

Euros. By 1ˢᵗ July, national currencies will no longer be legal tender, although redeemable at central banks. All retail transactions and payments across the economies of participating members will be carried out in Euros.

What is the UK's position?

On 16ᵗʰ October 1996 the UK government notified the European Council that it did not intend to move to stage 3 of EMU. To reverse this decision, the UK government needed to notify the European Council, before 1ˢᵗ January 1998, of its intent to join.

On 27ᵗʰ October 1997, the UK government announced that it would not join EMU during the first wave in 1999. The Maastricht Treaty allows for EU member states that have delayed joining EMU after the first phase. The UK, through its negotiated neutral position, will be one of these members, if it decides to opt in. Therefore, if the UK does not decide to join, it will have the opportunity to join at any time in the near future, subject to meeting a format of the convergence criteria.

So we can wait and see ?

Monetary union will affect every financial organisation within the UK on day one, 1ˢᵗ January 1999, even though the UK is not involved at that stage. Financial organisations across the City will be the most affected at this stage. Anyone that trades in the European equity markets or the European bond markets will be affected. However, in addition, it is possible that UK-registered organisations may be able to redenominate their share capital value into Euros and operate in them from this time too. This will mean that not only will European traders, and subsequently settlements be affected, but so too will UK traders and settlement. Already, multinationals such as Shell and Unilever are suggesting that they would move to such a position in order to reap the benefits of the reduction in currency exposure.

What are businesses currently doing in the UK?

In its *Practical Issues Arising from the Introduction of the Euro* the Bank of England presents a number of case studies of UK businesses currently considering the implications of EMU. These include Barclays Bank,

Midland Bank, and Marks and Spencer . These can be summarised in the following way:

Barclays Bank plc

Barclays have been preparing for the introduction of the Euro and have made the assumption that it will take place on 1st January 1999, initially without the participation of theUK. They have set up a Steering Committee, chaired by the Executive Director for Planning, Operations and Technology. The Committee's mandate is to oversee the direction of a Euro Programme. Below this Executive Committee is a Co-ordination Committee that is a forum for the exchange of ideas. They have set up working parties to discuss issues of common interest, such as settlements, cash management, foreign exchange, and so on. From this structure it has been possible for Barclays to set up short-term projects to develop and deliver group policies.

The role of the central group is to provide guidance and policy at a high level, but responsibility for assessment of the implications, determining requirements and setting implementation plans is down to individual business units.

As well as beginning to consider the implications for their working practices and supporting systems, Barclays have also begun to look at the effects EMU will have on their customers and the supply chain. To this end they have begun to allocate resources to consider likely changes and think of innovative ways to deal with them.

Midland Bank (HSBC)

Midland Bank have also put a programme structure in place to co-ordinate and manage their EMU preparations; these include:

- an executive steering committee
- an EMU programme management group
- a small number of full-time executives to co-ordinate IT-specific issues
- nominated managers in all major business lines and functions
- quarterly updates submitted to the board of directors.

Like Barclays, Midland (and HSBC) are actively investigating the implications of EMU for their business operations and supporting IT systems, and its effects on customers and suppliers.

Marks and Spencer

Marks and Spencer have retail operations throughout Europe. They are therefore currently considering the implications of EMU for their operations. They are assuming that retailers will be affected on 1st January 2002, when dual currencies are introduced. They also have the additional aspect of financial services to consider.

As well as considering the direct implications for their business practices and supporting systems they are also considering the likely behaviour of their customers. For one thing, they see the need to effectively communicate changes in order to reduce sceptism that it is just an excuse for a price increase. In fact, they are so focused on their customers' likely behaviour that one of their key objectives is 'to maintain the trust of customers, and to minimise the disruption to them and us'.

Like the examples from the financial sector, Marks and Spencer have formed a steering group, which is sponsored at board level. The steering committee is responsible for seeing the high-level, overall picture, reviewing progress and ensuring different business areas are locked into the process and understand the urgency of the situation.

Below the steering group is a full-time project manager, supported by a project team. Their role is to co-ordinate Marks and Spencer's plans, to implement changes and monitor day-to-day progress. As part of the project, all key business areas within Marks and Spencer are involved and are responsible for the investigation of their own areas, not least the IT department.

A common approach

Despite their differences in operation all of the three organisations described above have taken a similar approach to dealing with the EMU issue. They all have direction from board level, all have a steering committee and all have appointed a project/programme manager and project/programme team to specifically deal with this issue. A theme of this common strategic approach is presented in detail in Chapter 5. There are no specific 'one size fits all' answers to the issue. The approach presented, however, provides a framework for effectively dealing with it.

2 Business impacts

Fundamentally, the introduction of the Euro is a business issue that will have consequences for supporting systems. This chapter aims to identify the main concerns for business, the impacts on IT systems and information services providers are covered in later chapters.

Many people are unsure if EMU, and more specifically the introduction of the Euro, will affect them. EMU will affect UK business in two ways: whilst the UK remains outside of EMU we will face *Eurozone impacts* (January 1999–2002), but once we enter we will face *ultimate changes* (2002?).

Eurozone impacts are those that will impact on UK business as a result of the majority of the members of the European Union adopting the same currency. Instead of individual countries being defined by their national currency, EMU will create a trading sector defined by the Euro. These changes and their impacts will be felt from January 1999.

Ultimate changes, however, are those that UK business will have to make when, and if, the UK joins the Eurozone. Having said that, with organisations such as Rover opting to operate in the Euro before the UK joins it may be the case that some UK businesses will choose to either operate in the Euro altogether or run dual accounting, an option currently only favoured in Switzerland, due to its complexity.

This chapter focuses on the Eurozone impacts, especially on the financial sector (although it does cover some of the ultimate changes). It covers the European equity market, the UK equity market, European bonds, derivatives, settlement, custodian action and money market transactions.

European equity market

Pricing in the Euro

The main European stock markets have decided on a big bang approach to the introduction of the Euro. From 4th January 1999 they will all trade and quote in the Euro. This means that quotations displayed on traders' screens will be in Euros and transactions will be executed, recorded, matched, confirmed and passed to settlement in them.

In addition to those 11 countries entering into stage 3 quoting their equity prices in the Euro, the Swedish market is also considering such a move, whilst the London Stock Exchange is a multi-currency exchange offering pricing in over thirty currencies (see pp.20–22).

Redenomination of securities

On 1st January 1999 all shares, options and futures will be traded in one currency, the Euro. In general, companies need an EGM or AGM to change their capital structure, but because of its one-off nature and minor implications a general ruling may be given, thus allowing a redenomination at any time. If nothing is done during the transitional period redenomination will be done automatically by regulation during the first half of 2002.

It was concluded by an EU working party that non-par value (NVP) shares appear to be the easiest and least costly solution because they involve no physical share exchange. However, not all member states have passed legislation for this to happen, even though the EU's Second Company Law Directive allows it. The impact of this is that organisations' share capital values will gradually be redenominated to the Euro. Currently, the majority in the market place believe that a physical issue of new shares will be too costly and is not a realistic process to undertake.

There is likely to be a glut of redenominations at the beginning of the introduction of the Euro, with a steady trickle during 1999, decreasing in 2000 and finally picking up again in 2001. Examples of the different approaches being taken are Mercedes and Siemens. As stated in the

Introduction to this book, Mercedes have decided to change over to operating in the Euro from 1st January 1999. They will redenominate their share capital value into the Euro, pay their suppliers and staff in Euros, and offer their cars in Euros. Siemens, on the other hand, will wait for an AGM for permission to redenominate into the Euro. This is likely to be in September 1999. Many companies will take this kind of approach, redenominating at the earliest opportunity during 1999. Some, on the other hand, will wait until the latest opportunity and redenominate during 2001.

Renominalisation

The introduction of the Euro will also result in the restatement of authorised and issued share capital. Currently, issued share capital is generally stated in the national currency as being, for example: 100 IR£1 ordinary shares representing issued share capital of IR£100. After the introduction of the Euro this would be stated as 100 EUR1.2 ordinary shares representing issued share capital of Euro120. This will obviously have an impact on the way systems cope and holdings are reported.

Creation of the Eurozone

The emergence of the Eurozone is likely to be one of the major investment changes in the foreseeable future. There will be a shift from country to sector asset allocations in the longer term. As a result, equity risk characteristics will alter in a number of ways, including:

- reduced currency risk in the Eurozone
- increased correlation between EMU members.

Eurozone companies will experience a reduced currency risk because a greater proportion of their market will be in their base currency. This means that European investment will become more attractive and necessarily exert a gravitational pull on the UK market. The development of an equity culture will only add to this impetus and trading is likely to substantially increase within the European equity market. This change in characteristic must be considered at a strategic level within any investment organisation.

Benchmarks and reporting

Benchmarks currently in use will cease to be appropriate for Eurozone countries. National stock exchanges are likely to merge and in some cases disappear as EMU prompts greater competition between them. Company mergers are also likely to increase and convergence across the market is likely to further reduce the relevance of national listings. Currently, benchmark providers, such as FTSE International, are making pre-adjustments to their systems. Many are using ECU ratings as a proxy for fixing exchange rates, creating a synthetic Euro. This, in the case of FTSE, will provide a Eurozone index called 'the Euro-bloc'.

Paris, Zurich and Frankfurt stock exchanges have also joined forces to rival London's dominance with the introduction of a new index. They are to launch a 'Dow Jones Euro Stoxx 50', which will list blue chip firms in the Eurozone, including European Union countries and Switzerland. It is likely that a quarter of this new index will be made up of UK firms, by far the largest contribution of any country. In response to these changes, it is felt that there may be pressure on UK companies to quote in the Euro, creating a hybrid of the Eurozone benchmark.

Using benchmarks in a post-EMU world will therefore need to be a strategic consideration in the first place and consequently a business operational issue once a strategic decision has been made.

Impacts on front office spreadsheets

The majority of front office spreadsheets are based on country allocations and will therefore need to be changed in a fairly radical way. This will require careful analysis of what information is used and how it is processed. Spreadsheets held on Excel will need to be adjusted to take account of the fact that for those countries joining EMU their national legacy currencies will no longer exist. In addition, some countries under a European desk banner may not be entering into EMU, such as Switzerland, Sweden and Denmark. Where this is the case, an organisation must consider if this is the best way to continue allocating after the creation of the Eurozone.

A more important long-term issue relates to whether the UK is in or out of EMU. If the UK were to join, UK-based pension and insurance firms would necessarily move their base currency to the Euro. This would mean a likely shift of assets towards the European markets at the expense of the UK. Organisations must at least consider this within their long-term strategy even if they do not currently make any changes to their operations.

UK equity market

Whilst the UK remains outside of the Eurozone it is easy to think that the UK equity market will not be affected. However, the case is not so clear, since UK-based organisations are capable of quoting their price in Euros and will probably be allowed, through legislation, to redenominate their share capital value into the Euro.

Pricing in the Euro

The London Stock Exchange already has the capability of quoting prices in many different currencies. This is one of the reasons it has been so successful on a global level. When the Euro is introduced, it will be treated as any other currency. However, in reality, it is likely that many international organisations are likely to be priced in the Euro. For example, multinationals, such as Unilever and Shell, that are quoted on many exchanges will be priced in Euros. This will have implications for such things as spreadsheets, datafeeds, IT systems and dealer limits.

Redenomination of share capital whilst the UK is outside EMU

Whilst the UK is outside EMU, one of the main concerns will be the introduction of legislation to allow UK-based companies to redenominate their capital share value into the Euro and/or quote their share prices in Euros. This will have a number of implications for UK investment organisations:

- *dividends will be paid in Euros*: organisations must be able to receive dividends on this basis. Dividends paid in the Euro will generally be the exception to the rule until any decision is made about the UK joining. These could be handled on a one-off basis if they pose a problem to IT systems, although generally they can just be treated as any other foreign currency dividend.
- *currency exposure as a result of redenomination*: companies issuing new capital in Euros may expose an organisation to a currency risk upon

conversion. Ground rules for conversion will have to be established in order to minimise the performance impact.

- *share certificates*: there may be a legal requirement to replace existing share certificates if par values are redenominated, which will require a vast amount of effort. However, it is the intention of the London Stock Exchange and the Bank of England to place pressure on the government to allow for redenomination to take place on a no-par-value basis, without the physical exchange of certificates.
- *signatories*: objectives and constraints may have to be reviewed for UK signatories in order to allow them to deal in stocks with a Euro quote. Pension trustees must be asked for their permission to trade in Euro-denominated equity, since it is likely to be viewed as a Eurozone security, not a UK one.

Shift in asset allocation

As the European equity culture grows, more and more pressure will be placed on the UK market to join. The introduction of the Euro will make continental investment more attractive at an asset allocation level. This is likely to exert downward pressure on the UK market, and will raise an asset allocation issue.

The London Stock Exchange

The London Stock Exchange (LSE) is already a multi-currency trading platform, trading in 36 currencies. As a result, it will be able to support both sterling and the Euro for individual securities, should that be desired. Furthermore, if the UK does decide to join, UK companies will have the option of following the big bang approach to conversion or taking a more flexible approach. Whatever choice is made in the medium term, in the short term currency conversions will continue to be carried out by LSE member firms' in-house systems. Therefore, although some equities may be quoted in Euros and some in sterling, it is the responsibility of individual organisations to redenominate.

The LSE has also considered the denomination of a company's capital base for the listing and trading of securities. The choice of currency for trading and reporting does not depend on the currency in which the security is denominated; for example, securities that remain denominated in sterling can nevertheless be traded in Euros. The LSE expects that redenomination of share capital will be facilitated through

EMU-related legislation. Even though the UK is not joining in the first wave, the LSE supports the publication of legislation to facilitate redenomination through no-par value shares.

The London Stock Exchange has published a guide to the impacts of EMU at a glance and these can be summarised as:

- No change to trading rules and regulations.
- Facilities for Euro trading in securities to be available from 1999, with Euro trading in individual trading securities to be decided by the market.
- Orders left unexecuted over the changeover weekend will be cancelled.
- Exchange systems need no major changes.
- Intermediaries' systems continue to require facilities for currency conversion.
- Data on individual securities will be supplied by the exchange in the supported currency of trading.
- historical data will remain in sterling.

Impact on member firms and investors

- No changes to trading rules and regulations.
- Settlement and reporting systems to be enhanced to handle both currencies.
- Reporting of market statistics to remain in sterling.
- Exchange will work with relevant bodies to ensure that settlement is available in sterling and Euros.
- Currency of trading in UK securities to be determined by market demand.

Impact of EMU on listed companies

- No changes to listing rules.
- Redenomination of securities of companies wishing to use Euro.
- Redenominated securities issued with their original International Securities Identification Number (ISIN).

Impact on listing

- Under the Companies Act, UK-registered Public Limited Companies (PLCs) are required to have a minimum share capital of £50,000 denominated in sterling. The Exchange will support legislation to allow UK companies to qualify with equivalent share capital in Euros.

- No changes to the listing rules will be required, since multi-currency share capital is already permitted.
- Dividends can be paid in the currency of choice.

Market indices

- Pan-European indices will present European companies as forming one market. This, in turn, could lead to pressure to integrate trading across those countries.
- For companies, the threat of removal from a benchmark index, or the possibility of joining a new one, will have a considerable influence on whether and when they seek to redenominate shares.

The UK joins EMU

Any arrangements for countries joining after the first wave will be negotiated separately and there is a presumption that they should be allowed the same changeover period as those joining in phase 1. This means that the UK could be granted a two-year changeover period should the government feel that it is required.

When (or if) the UK participates in EMU, the case for sector rather than country specialisation will continue. This is a significant business issue for all UK investment companies. If the market sets a pan-European mandate and UK organisations are unable to respond to this on an active basis, it could result in them losing funds under management. Conversely the ability to meet this requirement could be a competitive advantage.

Bond markets

The bond markets are likely to see a greater impact at the beginning of 1999 compared to the equity markets. All new bond issues for joining countries will be in the Euro from 1st January 1999. In addition, many countries will choose to redenominate their existing debt over the conversion weekend.

The extent of corporate redenomination is still unclear. However, key market players believe that there will be some redenomination over the weekend, followed by a steady flow of redenomination over the transition period.

The introduction of the Euro is likely to make the European bond market more attractive to UK investors, with its increased liquidity. It may also be the case that the British government will start to issue national debt in the Euro in its attempt to move towards joining EMU and balancing the structure of the UK economy, by reducing the dominance of the equity market.

Redenomination of bonds

The EU believes that the early redenomination of sovereign debt is desirable, but not essential, for the transition from the use of national currencies to the use of the Euro. It stresses in its many reports that redenomination of a bond does not affect its value, only the way that it expressed.

Each of the joining governments will redenominate their national debt according to their own national law. There has been a general consensus that information relating to how countries are going to redenominate their debt should be made publicly available as soon as possible. The table below represents the information currently known.

Country	Debt to be Redenominated	Redenomination Basis	Rounding Rule	Minimum Nominal	New ISIN?
Austria	Only selected liquid government issues	Face value of each individual bond	Round to nearest Euro cent	One Euro cent	No
Belgium	Demateralised public debt securities: linear bonds (OLOS) and treasury certs	Investor holding (line by line in each investor account)	Round to nearest Euro cent	EUR1000 Odd lots of up to 999.99 will be repackaged	No
France	All negotiable government debt	Investor holdings	Round down to nearest Euro	One Euro, except OAT stripped coupons; 25 cents	Yes

Germany	Listed federal government bonds	Investor holdings	Round to nearest cent	One Euro cent	No
Ireland	General government debt	Investor holdings	Round to nearest cent	One Euro cent	No
Italy	Marketable government debt	Minimum nominal amount	Round to nearest cent	One Euro cent (may repackage)	No
Holland	All tradable government debt	Investor holdings	Round down to nearest cent	One Euro cent	Yes
Luxemburg	All demateralised linear bonds	Investor holdings	Round to nearest cent	One Euro cent	No
Portugal	Tradable government debt	Investor holdings	Probably round down to nearest cent	One Euro cent	No
Spain	All government debt registered at book entry system for government securities	Investor holdings	Round to nearest cent initially	EUR100 for government bonds and EUR10 for T-bills. Odd lots in Euro cents will be repackaged	No

The main points to note are that most governments intend to redenominate their existing debt. Also, most governments plan to redenominate to the nearest cent, whilst France has chosen the Euro and only France and Holland have chosen to issue new ISIN numbers.

Prospectus for future redenomination

Many Eurobonds are starting to include terms providing for redenomination into the Euro. In response to this trend, the International Primary Markets Association (IPMA) have made a number of recommendations; these include:

- Redenomination should only occur on an interest payment date.
- Interest payable on the interest payment date on which the bonds are redenominated should be payable in national legacy currency.
- Redenomination is at the issuer's option, it does not require bondholders' consent and requires 30 days' notice.
- If a bond is redenominated it should also be renominalised and the new harmonised market conventions should be applied.
- Where definitive notes are in circulation, the practicalities of renomilisation will need to be worked out by the paying agents and relevant clearing systems.
- Redenomination and renominalisation should be undertaken to the nearest cent.
- New ECU/Euro-style bond issues should provide for reconventioning from the first interest payment date after 1st January 1998.

Renominalisation of bonds

The minimal nominal amounts will have an impact on the way a bond is renominalised. For example, in the table on pages 23–24 it can be seen that the French and German governments have decided on different approaches and, consequently, the effects will be different.

Country	Original Issue	Conversion Rate	Redenomination	New Security Balance	Nominal Option
France	1,000,000	EUR 1 = 6.56789	1,000,000 / 6.56789 =	152255	Cash repayment: 0.90
Germany	1,000,000	EUR 1 = 1.98765	1,000,000 / 1.98765 =	503106.68	Decimal nominal value

The cash compensation will need to be accounted for by the owner of the issue. It is expected that corporates will follow the same option as their government, i.e. French organisations will take the option to give a cash repayment rather than use the decimal route.

Reconvention of existing bonds

All new issues will follow a standard convention for the Euro: of an actual/actual day count basis, the use of decimals for bond quotations and settlement days of trade plus 3. ISDA and IPMA have produced documents consistent with these agreed market conventions. Already many EU countries, including the UK, have agreed to them and others are likely to agree during the first half of 1998.

Where a country has not previously operated on this basis it may choose to change the conventions for its existing debt. This would obviously cause an impact on accrued interest calculations, maturity dates, and so on. It is likely that the majority of joining countries will take this opportunity to reconvention their debt.

Ratings

It is expected that the introduction of the Euro will cause a shift in ratings, which will be allocated by agencies such as IBCA, Poor's and Moody's. The main benefit for organisations is that it is likely that the Eurozone will have a 'sovereign ceiling' rating of AAA, which will mean that, once the Euro is seen to be stable, corporates and banks within a country will no longer be constrained by that country's rating. However, the rating of member state governments is unlikely to change in the immediate future and will reflect current ratings of AAA, AA+, AA and AA-.

The convergence of the spot rates over the last few years has shown the move towards harmonisation of credit-risk assessment across the European market. When the Euro is introduced, currency will be removed as a risk factor. However, no government will be risk free because of the 'no bail out clause' of the EMU members. Country ratings will therefore stay in place and will be used for government debt.

Changes to ISIN numbers

The issue of International Securities Identification Numbers (ISINs) is governed by rules set by the Association of National Numbering Agencies (ANNA). Current guidelines already allow for single issues with different denominations. New ISINs are only required when the new denomination is not fungible with the security formerly available. If an entire issue of securities is fungible, redenomination of a security to the Euro will not affect the rights of the holder. In this case, the fungibility is maintained and there is no reason to create a new ISIN. This, in fact, has been the recommendation of the ANNA.

However, whilst most countries have decided to follow this principle, France and Holland have not. This means that systems will have to cope with redenomination in two ways: for those ISIN that do not change after redenomination and those that do.

Business days, hours and recruitment implications

This concerns the difference between UK and European working hours and personnel requirements. Eurozone trading will take place between 8am and 6pm Frankfurt time. This will obviously have an impact on UK-based organisations. Those organisations that wish to continue trading throughout the day must provide staff to cover the market's opening times.

Portfolio characteristics

As a result of harmonisation across the European market, there will be major shifts in the characteristics of portfolios. This must be a consideration of any investor. Where once there may have been eleven currencies to consider there will now be only one: the Euro. Organisations must take a strategic decision on whether they want to become more exposed to this increased liquid market or less exposed.

Benchmarks

As for the equity market, there will be a need for new benchmarks from January 1999. There are likely to be pan-European indices and Eurozone indices. Some will incorporate the UK and other countries, such as Switzerland, whilst others will not. Organisations must investigate any changes that will be implemented and their impact on business operations and strategy.

Derivatives

There will be a number of impacts on derivative markets once the Euro is introduced in January 1999. The International Swaps and Derivatives Association Inc. (ISDA) present a number of impacts that include:

- It is expected that all transactions dealt in the interbank market after 1st January 1999 will be traded in the Euro.
- New transactions executed with corporates are expected to be increasingly denominated in the Euro. However, smaller corporates and retail counterparties may continue to be traded in a national legacy currency until later in the transition period.
- The new market conventions will apply from 1st January 1999 across the Euro bond market, money market, foreign exchange and related derivative markets. These changes include harmonisation in the money markets: of the day count basis across Europe to Actual/360, two day spot as standard settlement basis and a two-day rate fixing convention as the fixing period for derivative contracts. The harmonisation of bond market conventions: of an actual/actual day count basis, the use of decimals for bond quotations and settlement days of trade plus 3. Finally, there will be new conventions for the foreign exchange markets: of a two-day standard spot settlement basis and quotations of certain for uncertain (1 Euro = n foreign currency).

BBA LIBOR

The British Bankers Association (BBA) has already expressed its intention to provide a EUR-LIBOR-BBA quotation based on a similar quotation, calculation and reference panel to those LIBOR rates currently calculated. Specifically, the BBA announced that EUR LIBOR will replace XEU LIBOR from 1st January 1999 and the fixing of the BBA LIBOR will take place at 11am London time.

Transitional legacy deals

Some derivative-based products issued before the start of stage 3 will not mature until after the end of the transitional period in 2002. This means that when they mature the initial currency they were denominated in will no longer exist. The regulations laid down by the EU suggest that there will not be any force applied to make counterparties redenominate their derivative portfolios *en masse*. It is expected that the general market practice will be to continue to record derivative transactions in their original national currency, together with their original terms and conditions. Whilst the nominal values of most derivatives will remain unchanged, and the key terms unaltered, it is likely that some elements of the contract may have to change. This will happen where the underlying price will disappear, or where there is a change in the strike price for equity derivatives or for the underlying asset in the case of bond options on government debt.

In order to redenominate a derivative product both counterparties must agree to the changes. Where this does occur, it is likely that only the nominal value of the derivative will change, affecting only the notional amount and the interest payments. The underlying parameters of the transaction should remain the same, including the calendar used for day-count fractions and payments schedules.

Market conventions will also apply to existing legacy instruments entered into before the introduction of the Euro. Even if a derivative switches to a new price source, existing conventions will be retained. There will therefore be some differences between some derivatives: for example, BEF money markets operate on an Actual/365 basis, whilst the Euro will operate on an Actual/360 basis.

The maintenance of conventions will have a number of implications:

- Firstly, information service providers will have to supply Euro quotes on existing conventions to cope with changes in the notional value and interest payments, but not to the convention.
- Systems will need to be able to handle Euro-denominated quotes on both new and old conventions.

Business days for settlement and rate fixing for Euro transactions will also be different. The result could be that the economics of a transaction and its hedge could diverge. The easiest way to avoid such events would be to continue with the original convention.

Cross-currency swaps of Euro:Euro derivatives

Another consideration that needs to be made is where transactions no longer serve any economic purpose as a result of EMU. For example, FFvDM cross-currency swaps will no longer have a purpose with the introduction of the Euro and organisations will need to take a strategic decision as to what action they will take to rationalise their portfolios.

Settlement arrangements

Article 8 of the EU regulations means that counterparties in a derivative transaction have full freedom to start making Euro payments or request the conversion of any incoming payments into the Euro from 1st January 1999, without any need to inform counterparties of the new arrangements. The article firmly puts the burden of conversion on commercial banks. However, this does not apply to rate resets and payment advices. To change these, agreement between counterparties is required.

Transactions denominated in the ECU

All existing references to the ECU will be replaced by the Euro on a one for one basis. No redenomination or conversion is required, since this is facilitated through the EU regulations. However, there will be some implications of this action. For example, XEU LIBOR will be succeeded by a EUR LIBOR and the XEU PIBOR will be replaced by the Euro EURIBOR.

Forward Euro deals

Some market participants may wish to enter in forward Euro deals before the start of EMU, whereby contracts refer explicitly to the Euro. Where this is the case, ISDA recommend that deals are booked on an ECU basis. However, care should be taken to ensure that one of the new price sources would apply once the Euro is introduced.

However, it may be that after the bilateral rates are announced in May 1998 Euro settlement arrangements may be available. This will have implications for an organisation's supporting information systems. Care should be taken to ensure that deal entry, settlement and accounting functions can take place.

LIFFE

LIFFE has made extensive preparations for the introduction of the Euro to ensure its futures and options contracts remain at the forefront of the derivatives market. Their main strategy has been to review and enhance their existing product range and to develop its technology platforms to support its open outcry trading environment.

In particular, they believe that their five Short Term Interest Rate (STIR) contracts will be hugely affected: three-month Euro futures, one-month Euromark futures, three-month Euromark futures and options, three month Eurolira futures and options and Short Sterling (three-month) futures and options.

In response, they have made a number of provisions:

- *Settlement price*: Contract specifications have been made so that the Euromark, Eurolira, Euro and Short Sterling futures contracts will settle against the BBA Euro LIBOR interest rate for short-term deposits, if the NCUs (National Currency Units) are for 'in' currencies.
- *Conventions*: Whilst recommendations have been made to rationalise the day-count and fixing-value period to actual/360, T+2 across the Euro money markets, LIFFE believe that it remains unclear which conventions will be implemented and they have catered for both. Day count has made legal provisions in its contracts to ensure the settlement rate of its STIR contracts reflects the current national day count convention. This means that the settlement of the Short Sterling contract will probably continue to be based on actual days/365. However, the legal aspects of their contract allow for a change to an actual/360 convention using BBA Euro LIBOR.
- To maintain the value date of a contract, the LTD of a contract will be altered if the fixing-value period in the Euro cash deposit market differs from that of the national currency on which the contract was based.
- *Conversion facilities – Spread Trading Facility (STF) and Voluntary Position Conversion (VPC)*: These two mechanisms have been designed by LIFFE to allow for the smooth transition to the formulation of the Euro benchmark.

For further information, see their Website: www.liffe.com.

Spreadsheet changes

Live derivative positions opened prior to 1st January 1999 will remain in their legacy currency. New positions, however, will be opened in the Euro. This means that systems, i.e. spreadsheets, need to be able to handle both legacy currencies and the Euro, until all positions are held in

Euros. It may also be necessary to amalgamate the positions to provide a total exposure.

Analysis is necessary to assess the time and resources required to make the necessary spreadsheet changes.

Back office operations

One of the implications of the introduction of the Euro is that quotations in participating countries will be displayed in Euros. Transactions will be executed, recorded, matched, confirmed and transmitted to settlement in Euros. Furthermore, all inter-market operations will be conducted in Euros. This will leave the financial intermediaries to make the conversions needed for processing by their clients.

Transactions undertaken in a national currency on or before 31st December 1998 would be settled in Euros on the agreed date. Unexecuted orders remaining in a central order execution system over the transition weekend (31st December 1998–4th January 1999) would be cancelled. In order for these orders to be executed they would have to be converted to Euros and reintroduced.

Physical redenomination of securities

Actually redenominating a stock on a back office system will be time consuming and resource intensive. Operations are likely to be affected in three major ways: before the conversion weekend, over the weekend and post-weekend. Leading up to 4th January 1999, the first Euro trading day, back office will have to put business processes in place to cope with the introduction of the Euro. They will also have to work in partnership with IT people to ensure that technical systems can cope with the changes in business processes.

It is likely that custodians and other sources of information will provide market participants with details of redenomination, reconventions and renominalisation. For example, earlier in this chapter (pp23–4) details relating to the redenomination of government debt are outlined in a table. This information should be reviewed and used in planning work before and during the conversion weekend. Assumptions can be made and tasks can be scheduled.

Rounding differences and cash repayments

If organisations follow the advice of the Bank of England, they will undertake an end of year reconciliation on 31st December, confirm this with the custodians before conversion, undertake conversion once the rates are known and then do another reconciliation after the weekend. This will allow them to spot any differences.

Custodians must, by law, take account of rounding differences, since they do not own the underlying security, and, as a result, are likely to set up an account for rounding differences.

They will therefore make a cash repayment for any rounding differences that occur as a result of redenomination. At the moment, it is not clear whether these will be liable to tax or can be written off and donated to charity. However, some organisations may want, or may have to, carry out an audit to find the exact places where differences occurred. It may cost more money to find the small differences than the actual cash repayment, since cash repayments are likely to be small (a few thousand, rather than hundreds of thousands).

Changing ISIN numbers

As suggested previously, there is likely to be a need to change some ISIN numbers. Currently, only the French and Dutch have stated that they will make changes. This means physical changes within a system. This will require time and effort from back office personnel, which should be planned for during any Euro project.

Official changes to ISIN numbers will be known before the fourth quarter of 1998 and, once known, a review of the impact of this should be undertaken. It sounds like this will cause a vast amount of work. However, the reality is that it may only mean physically changing a few lines within a system; an organisation might only hold a dozen French Bonds.

Nostro accounts

The introduction of one currency across Europe will allow organisations to consolidate their nostro accounts. However, whilst this is not a problem for new deals, it poses a problem for existing contractual obligations to send payments to specified accounts. Therefore, organisations will have to maintain their existing nostro accounts for the immediate future. If they aim to move to rationalise their accounts, they must agree with their counterparties to change arrangements. This should be done with at least 30 days' notice.

Custodians are likely to set up new Euro-based accounts and link national legacy currency accounts to them. They will then sweep balances of national legacy currencies into these accounts and apply one interest rate across them. It will then be the decision of the custodian's client as to when to close the old accounts. As each account requires reconciliation and auditing the move to one nostro account would be advantageous and should be aimed for at the earliest opportunity.

Custodians

The Global Custodians' EMU Forum was formed at the end of 1997. Its purpose is to provide a clear and unified statement to the markets on how global custodians and their clients should operate in a post-Euro world. The Forum consists of representatives from The Bank of New York, Bankers Trust, Brown Brothers Harriman, Chase Manhattan, Citibank, Lloyds Bank, Mellon Trust, Midland Bank, Morgan Stanley, Northern Trust, RBS Trust, Royal Trust and State Street.

At a strategic level, the Forum recommend that a big bang approach to security and cash processing is adopted. This approach represents a comprehensive conversion of wholesale market securities and related cash activity to the Euro as of the conversion weekend. The Forum go further and make a number of recommendations:

1. Global custodians should accept settlement instructions up to normal cut-off times on 30th December 1998. In exceptional circumstances, and through agreement with a custodian and their client, instructions may be accepted in the national legacy currency on 31st December.
2. Custodians should make statements of positions available on 31st December.
3. Custodians should liaise with their clients and complete a reconciliation of their position and document any discrepancies.
4. The conversion process should commence as soon as practicable after the reconciliation process is complete, with the aim of completion by midday on 2nd January 1999.
5. Cash accounts will need to be converted to the Euro or new accounts set up.

6. Securities will be redenominated to the Euro and assigned new ISIN numbers in accordance with the practices laid down by member countries.

7. In order to facilitate securities processing across the market a part of any holding less than one Euro of nominal value should be disposed of at the point of redenomination.

8. Open trades should be converted to reflect settlement in the Euro without the need for renotification, rematching or reinstruction to the market.

9. After the conversion weekend, custodians should make statements of positions available to clients.

10. Custodians should reconcile post-Euro statements with their clients and document any differences. Any differences should equate to those documented in the reconciliation process conducted prior to conversion and redenomination. This should be completed before the end of play on 3rd January 1999.

Announcement of the conversion rates

Currently, there are no fixed plans on how and when the conversion rates are to be announced on 31st December 1998.

Further investigation needs to take place. Organisations need to gain an understanding from the market – who will announce the conversion rates? How will they be announced? and at what time will they be announced? Will custodians pass this through? Will it be a market-wide announcement?

Resourcing the weekend

The back office will be the most impacted area over the conversion weekend. The work that will need to be undertaken over this period includes:

- reconciliation of end of year position
- entering fixed conversion rates
- re-pricing of securities
- redenomination of government debt
- renominalisation of government debt and handling of nominal amounts
- make changes to French and Dutch ISIN numbers

- redenomination of some corporate debt
- redenomination of some equities
- management of outstanding transactions
- reconciliation after the conversion process
- compare the post- and pre-conversion period
- open for trade and confirmation.

Corporate actions

It is likely that most decisions to redenominate and renominalise will be communicated as a corporate action. Leading up to the conversion weekend this is likely to come in dribs and drabs as more information becomes available and more and more organisations make a decision to redenominate. However, after the conversion, and for the next three and a half years, organisations will receive information on a regular basis as organisations elect to swap over to the Euro. Once again information relating to redenomination and renominalisation will be passed to them via corporate actions. Where this is the role of the custodian, information will probably be sent to a client on a weekly basis. Like many things, though, the exact details of how this might be done are unconfirmed. It might be that custodians send a disk weekly with forthcoming changes, release the data on the Internet or put it in a written bulletin. Organisations must confirm with whoever will supply them with this information as to what format it will be received in and on what basis.

Stock lending

The complexities involved in trying to redenominate and renomilise lent stock will be considerable. In order to make the changes required the best thing a lending organisation can do is to call back the stock. This will have contractual and physical implications that must be considered and managed as part of a continuing Euro programme.

There will be a few cases where stock will need to be recalled before the conversion weekend. However, there will be many more occasions in the future where stock must be returned as organisations choose to redenominate. If organisations participate in stock lending then they must consider this as part of their overall analysis and should develop a strategy to deal with these events.

Money market transactions

From 4th January 1999 the wholesale money markets will operate in the Euro. It will still be possible to undertake partial or full transaction in a national legacy currency, although this will be the exception, rather than the norm.

This section presents the intentions of key market players, such as Euroclear, CREST and CHAPS Euro.

Settlement

Most transactions will settle in the Euro; consequently, counterparties in Europe will set up settlement systems in Euros and therefore organisations do not need to convert to Euros themselves. However, they must be prepared to accept that transactions in the Eurozone will move to operating in the Euro only.

At present DM Interbank deposit rates are quoted for, say, one month DM, on information feeds and automated broking screens. Unless otherwise stated, these quotations are for value on the second Frankfurt business day after the spot day. The maturity date is for the same day, the next month, unless that is not a trading day. In the latter case it would be the next day of business, unless this was in the next month, when it would be the day before.

When a deal has been struck, the receiving bank advises the paying bank of the bank account in Frankfurt to which the funds are to be paid. The paying bank instructs its correspondent in Frankfurt via SWIFT to make the payment via the German payments system. Prior to maturity, the depositing bank advises its counterparty about the bank in Frankfurt to which the deposit is to be repaid. This amount is interest charged for the month calculated on the basis of the actual number of days from the spot date to the date of maturity (counting one of the two days) divided by 360. The deposit-taking bank instructs its correspondent in Frankfurt via SWIFT to make payment via the German payments system.

In the UK, Interbank sterling one-month quotations in London are for value that day. The paying bank usually sends the payment directly to the receiving bank's account via CHAPS. The interest is calculated using a divisor of 365.

After 1st January 1999, Euro deposits will be available for same-day value as well as for value on the second London business day after the spot day. This requires clarity in the terms being quoted and attention to the value date when transactions are concluded, recorded and confirmed.

The basis of interest calculation will be the actual number of days from value to maturity divided by 360. The receiving bank will be able to request payment of Euros to its account in London or Frankfurt. The paying bank will then have a choice of how to pay. If it has a London-based bank account it can initiate payment directly via CHAPS Euro. If it has a bank account in Frankfurt it will have to instruct its correspondent in Frankfurt, via SWIFT, to make payment via the German RTGS or net settlement system. Alternatively, it can initiate payment directly via the link between CHAPS Euro and TARGET.

TARGET

TARGET (Trans-European Automated Real-Time Gross Settlement Express Transfer System) has been cited as the most impressive option for the transmission of the Euro, offering the potential for banks to make same-day credit transfers to the majority of banks in the EU.

TARGET is a product of the EMI (European Monetary Institute) who see it linking to the European Real-Time Gross Settlement Systems. Behind its development are the central European banks who believe that it will offer an impressive tool for making fast and efficient payments in Euros. The main points of its operation can be summarised as:

- TARGET will operate on a central European Time, 7am–6pm.
- TARGET will operate on all weekdays except Christmas Day and New Year's Day.
- There will be a cross-border price for TARGET transfers, determined by the European Central Bank (ECB). This is likely to be 1.5–3 EUR, based on the principle of full recovery.
- TARGET will have its control and procedures provided by the ECB.
- National RTGS systems will take part in market-wide testing during 1998, finishing in the fourth quarter of that year.
- The Bank of England has stated that UK commercial banks will be able to make and receive TARGET payments.
- SWIFT has agreed a contract with the EMI to supply its core FIN message processing system and network as a communication link between the central banks participating in TARGET.

CHAPS Euro

In respect of CHAPS, the UK system, a number of assumptions can be made:

- CHAPS Euro will be available for wholesale payments within the UK and cross-border to and from the UK at the start of stage 3 of EMU from 4th January 1998.
- CHAPS Euro will operate alongside the sterling RTGS system.
- CHAPS Euro will allow both domestic payment between its members and between its members and other European RTGS systems through TARGET.
- CHAPS Euro will be available every day that TARGET is.
- CHAPS Euro will be a two-tiered operation, with settlement members and participants, but there is likely to be an increase in the number of direct participants compared to CHAPS sterling (around 300 indirect access participants).
- CHAPS Euro is being developed to handle any of the options for intra-day credit that are currently being raised.

Euroclear

The Euroclear real-time settlement system will be launched during 1998. It will increase same-day turnaround capabilities and offer competitive deadlines and maximised settlement efficiency with reduced settlement risk. Euroclear will allow participants to use it as a central hub for cross-border settlement activity.

More and current information can be found on Euroclear's Internet Web page: www.euroclear.com.

From 1st January 1999 income, redemption and other custody proceeds on securities denominated in an EMU currency, ECU or Euro will be paid exclusively in Euros (unless a non-EMU currency option is specified in the terms and conditions of the issue).

Euroclear offers multi-currency settlement in either Euro, a local European currency or any other Euroclear settlement currency. Both parties must agree and input instructions with the same settlement currency and the cash amount will remain matching elements.

The same features as for settlement within the Euroclear system will apply to Bridge instructions. (See Chapter 4.)

From 1st January 1999 income and redemption proceeds and tax refunds on securities denominated in an EMU currency, Euro or ECU will be paid in Euros. Entitlement payments will no longer be made in the local currency.

Participants will be able to use the Euroclear Money Transfer service as they do today, with the Euro as the new currency, alongside EMU currencies. However, for simplification, participants are likely to decide to convert their EMU currency balances into Euros.

Euroclear will automatically convert ECU cash balances into Euros by 4th January 1999. They will provide same-day conversion possibilities from EMU currencies into the Euro and vice versa and they will also extend the range of money transfer services to the Euro.

CREST

CREST already settles in both sterling and Irish pounds and will support settlement of transactions in US dollars from autumn 1998. In addition, they will be able to offer full equity and bond settlement in the Euro from 1st January 1999. Clients will be required to undertake conversion should they hold a sterling account only.

Each security will have one currency quotation and the decision to switch security trades to the Euro will be decided by the London or Irish Stock Exchanges respectively.

SWIFT message systems

Earlier this year SWIFT issued guidelines on how their messages should be used during the process of conversion to the Euro: *SWIFT Guide, Converting to the Euro*. This document covers EMU in general, issues relating to standards and a number of scenarios that cover payment, securities, treasury and trade and finance. For a copy of the guide contact SWIFT at euro@swift.com.

This document suggests that the introduction of the Euro will have limited impact on SWIFT. In summary, the EUR code will be introduced into the system and a mechanism for introducing the Euro-Related Information (ERI), e.g redenomination, renominalisation, and so on, will be implemented. Specific technical guidelines and standards have been published and should be consulted.

In this section a summary of the main participants in the wholesale money market has been presented. Further details are presented in the Bank of England's *Practical Issues Arising from the Introduction of the Euro*.

Alternatively, additional and up-to-date information can be obtained from contacting these bodies directly.

Accounting

The main implications of the introduction of the Euro for UK accounting systems are that they will have to cope with the introduction of the new currency and its replacement of existing national currencies. This will have system implications for the conversion of currencies, and so on, as outlined in Chapter 3.

From 1st January 1999, finance departments will need to convert European currency balances to the Euro – including dividends receivable and broker balances – in line with changes made on their main IT systems and the external markets.

Taxation

It is not expected that EMU will create any new forms of tax liability, although a cash repayment may be viewed as income and will therefore be liable to tax.

Conversion of base currency to the Euro

It is not expected that many UK companies will convert their base currency to the Euro whilst the UK remains outside of EMU. Some organisations with strong European ties may decide to run in dual currencies. However, the complexities of running dual currencies may put people off.

If and when the UK joins, the base currency for all accounting purposes will have to be converted. The timing of this will be dependent on individual organisations. Generally, it will be sensible to move to using the Euro when an organisation chooses to redenominate this share capital into the Euro.

3 Impacts on supporting IT systems

The impact of the introduction of the Euro on the IT systems of any financial organisation will be dependent on the business decisions taken to deal with the introduction of the new currency. Whilst these are specific to every project they will all have common aspects. Below is a summary of some of the top ten issues:

1. A system must be able to calculate foreign exchanges to six significant figures.
2. Conversion of currencies must only be by division, multiplying the inverse is not acceptable.
3. Where a result of an exchange is 0.5 of a Euro cent or more, it must be rounded up.
4. Conversion of sterling (or any other 'out' currency) must first be denominated into the Euro before being exchanged with any national legacy currency, e.g. DM or FF.
5. A system must be able to use the ISO standard 'EUR' symbol for the Euro.
6. A system must be able to input an exchange rate to six decimal places.
7. Nominal values of bonds will have to be held to 2 decimal places.
8. Exchange rates will be quoted with the Euro as the primary currency, i.e. £0.7 to one Euro.

9. The redenomination of bonds may cause a discrepancy in the value that will result in a cash payment to the bearer.
10. Some equity holdings of 'in' countries will need to be redenominated over the conversion weekend.

For a further detailed analysis, a simple model can be considered when undertaking a review of the impact of the introduction of the Euro on IT systems:

Inputs – Processing – Outputs

Each part of the process is now taken separately.

Input problems

Inputs come from a variety of areas, but specifically information service providers. These must be reviewed as part of any IT impact analysis and any changes must be incorporated into a further design and development stage.

Security prices

One of the first implications of the introduction of the Euro will be an immediate change to the quotation prices of 'in' countries. Once the Eurozone begins operating on 4th January 1999, organisations will need to be able to process Euro prices from external sources.

Exchange rates

Currently, most systems report exchange rates against the system's base currency. Following the start of EMU, rates will need to be quoted between the Euro and the base currency. The legacy national currency will need to be incorporated as a static conversion rate.

Internal processing problems

The internal processing of information within a system will be affected by its external feeds, deal entry, output requirements, the needs of interfacing systems and the impact of redenominating existing valuations, especially in respect of the regulations for converting joining countries' currencies.

Conversion of currencies

One of the main problems organisations will face is the conversion of legacy currencies into the Euro. This must follow the guidelines laid down by the European Commission in Regulation 235. Bird and Bird, the specialist IT lawyers, have provided a paper on the legal implications of EMU and summarise the conversion to the Euro and rounding.

The conversion rate will be based on one Euro expressed in terms of each participating national currency to six significant figures. This does not mean six decimal places. The Bank of England has adopted an hypothetical example as follows:

1 Euro = £0.765432 or FF6.58001 or DM0.192003

The Commission has said that the conversion rate may not be truncated or rounded so it could not be shortened to FF6.58. Systems must take account of this ruling within their processing of Euro-related data.

If the result of the actual conversion adopted on 1ˢᵗ January 1999 is not an exact number then it will be rounded up or down to the nearest sub-unit. If this produces a result exactly half way, this sum will be rounded up.

The conversion from one participating national currency unit to another during the transitional period must involve a three-step, triangular process:

1. conversion to the Euro from the first national currency at the fixed conversion rate with the result being rounded to not less than three decimal places
2. conversion of the resulting amount in the Euro to the second currency at the relevant fixed conversion rate
3. rounding the final result to the nearest sub-unit.

This can be summarised as:

national currency A (e.g. DM) – convert to Euro (to three decimal places) – convert to national currency B (e.g. FF).

The Commission has stated that the method is not the most important thing: the result is more important. If a system can produce the same outcome through another, perhaps easier process, then this can be used.

Conversion of national legacy currencies to sterling will require that they are converted to the Euro first. This must be considered within the processing of any system.

If the decision is taken to restrict inputs to the Euro, then the rounding will follow a normal Euro/sterling conversion. In this case, the Euro will be like any other foreign currency. Exchange processes can then be undertaken in a normal manner. However, where inputs are still received in the national legacy currency a work around must be put in place.

The use of decimals

The practicalities of redenominating national currency values into the Euro will mean showing nominal values to two decimal places. Systems must be able to accommodate the use of decimals.

Changes to SEDOL and ISIN numbers

Additional impacts are the changes that will be made to SEDOL and ISIN numbers. France and Holland have announced that they will change their ISIN numbers for existing debt that is redenominated. Systems must be able to take any changes into account, tracking them where necessary for audit purposes.

Problems with information in the database

Assets currently within a portfolio are usually held on a central database. The redenomination of values on any database, where values are expressed as national legacy currencies, will require functional changes to a system, in order that they may be expressed in Euros. The conversion of currencies must follow the triangular routine laid down by the European Commission if they are to be converted to sterling (see above), which may require changes in the current routines within systems and/or additional ones.

Dealer limits

Another area that may be affected is dealer limits. If limits use national currencies of joining states they will require conversion to the Euro. Authorisation of transactions over certain dealer limits will need to be reviewed because of the creation of one single market. Amongst other things, validation checks of value, e.g. on value range, will also be affected if used on these currencies; broker limits and currencies will need to be changed.

ISO standard – EUR

The currency code for the Euro has been agreed as 'EUR'. Any reference to the Euro in systems must use this ISO standard. This will require changes in the internal processing of the system and input and output functionality.

Standing data

The use of standing data within systems, in particular a central database, must also be considered. If an organisation chooses to operate in the Euro only, then data that is currently held in national currencies will need to be converted into the Euro. This may be a one-off event or it may be a continual process, depending on the requirements of the system. This will not only impact on the database, but will also have an impact on any interfacing applications such as Electronic Trade Confirmation and Accounting packages.

One of the key changes will be made in the number of days of trading and the opening hours of European exchanges, including LIFFE and LSE; these will affect calendar dates within a system.

There may also need to be changes made to fields containing information about clients and brokers.

Income tax table standing data will need to be set up or changed for the Euro. This will have an impact on dividends.

There are certain areas that can be updated prior to 1st January 1999 once we are in possession of the information: i.e. currency code set-up, currency added to brokers, parameters and tables, sectors and analysis codes.

Historical data

Since sterling will continue to be the base currency of most UK organisations, historical data will be required in that currency. Where systems store historical data relating to national legacy currencies of joining countries a conversion will be needed if that information is required for processing.

Since the Euro is a new currency there is no natural history. In order to be able to continue to provide historical price evaluations a work around is required. One way would be to produce a synthetic history, or something similar, based on a basket of 'in' currencies or converting all historical data at today's exchange rates. An organisation must consider its need for historical data and whether the importance of knowing past positions is enough to warrant extensive work. Further guidance on this issue will be made available by the Bank of England and the EU during 1998.

Brokers

The new currency will need to be added to all relevant brokers to enable dealing to commence. Counterparty limits will not be affected as these are usually set in sterling regardless of deal currency.

Valuation changes as a result of a movement to sector analysis

Valuations will need to be restructured to reflect new sectors and country code: i.e. Pan-European. This will involve moving stocks from national currency sectors to new sectors and changing existing analysis codes for reporting purposes. This also encompasses geographic location, which will need a flag added to indicate 'EMU'.

Country of origin based on currency information

If any systems pick up the country of origin based on that country's currency, they will be impacted by the introduction of the Euro on 1st January 1999. The business must make a decision about how it wishes to handle such changes.

Output problems

Outputs from systems, from valuation reports to custodian links, will be impacted by the introduction of the Euro. In summary, the problems associated with outputs are as follows.

Displays and reporting

During the transitional period users may require the display and reporting of dual currencies for joining member states, since many organisations will still be operating in their national legacy currencies. The requirement for this will need to be ascertained from the users. If they decide that they require dual currency display it poses a number of problems:

- Displaying information on forms, screens, reports, and so on may be difficult due to lack of space.
- Functionality must be added to make systems capable of doing this. This includes full reporting of sub-totals and totals which may be subject to rounding problems.

Even if they do not require dual prices and move over to the use of the Euro, changes will be required to displays and reports. This will require substantial functional system changes. Users must be consulted as to what exactly their requirements are, focusing on those aspects that are business critical.

Having said that, it is likely that the majority of UK companies will trade in the Euro from 1st January 1999, rather than in national legacy currencies, to reflect the general approach in the wholesale market. Custodians and counterparties are also likely to follow this pattern.

Financial modelling

Where information from a system is used for financial modelling the impact of the introduction of the Euro must be considered. Where national legacy currencies are no longer used but the Euro is, it will require changes in functionality. The requirements of users, both internal and external, must be fully considered and system changes made to reflect their developing needs.

Custodian links

An organisation may require the information received and sent to the custodians to be changed. Custodians are currently working together in the form of the Global Custodians' Forum to decide on market-wide recommendations. These recommendations are considered in an earlier section (p.33). Any impacts must be incorporated into any system changes.

Interface problems

Interfaces and messaging systems must be able to cope with any system changes both in terms of IT and information service providers. Care must be taken to ensure that information systems are talking about the same currency. There have been several warnings about the closeness of the Euro in value to the pound and DM.

In addition, the timings of changes must be co-ordinated to ensure that they are made together.

PC software

As well as impacts on investment management systems, there will be impacts on more general software and hardware.

Microsoft products

The Euro, €, is a new character that will have to be implemented within existing computer operating systems. Many companies are now dependent on Microsoft Office products. The Euro symbol can be used within the Office products; however, it must be presented as a graphic symbol. Currently, Microsoft products do not *fully* support the use of the Euro currency symbol.

Microsoft offer advice on the readiness of their product to handle the Euro and, in particular, how to install the Euro sign in all of their Office products. This advice can be downloaded from the Internet from premium.microsoft.com/support/office/content/tahoma/euro.asp.

User developed spreadsheets

User developed spreadsheets will be impacted where any of the 11 joining currencies are used. Analysis of the general impacts should be undertaken and a statement made about the generic implications.

If UK-based organisations redenominate their share capital value into Euros, there will be an impact on the spreadsheets held by the UK desk. Spreadsheets currently denominated in pounds may have to be amended. All key applications should be checked and signed-off by the end of September 1998.

New hardware

Any new hardware purchases should consider the impact of the Euro and, in particular, the impact of the new Euro symbol. Companies such as Compaq and DEL have indicated that they currently have no plans to incorporate the new Euro symbol. It is recommended that hardware suppliers are constantly contacted until they can provide answers.

Impacts on new systems

It is apparent from the above information that co-operation is essential between project managers overseeing the implementation of new products involved in a Euro project. In the immediate future, 1999–2002, IT systems must be able to support the use of the Euro for those currencies entering into EMU. This must be considered as part of any project.

Once, or if, the UK joins, probably in 2002, new systems must be able to support the conversion of sterling into the Euro. This will require considerable changes to IT systems, especially in the accounting area. In order to minimise any long-term additional costs, the purchase of new products must take the longer-term issues into account. (See chapter 7.)

4   Impacts on information service providers

Information service providers will have a large influence on business processing and IT systems. The way information is presented and the strategic decisions a business takes will be influenced by the information received. Below are a number of summaries of major information service providers. These are only summaries of information they have made publicly available. Where known, their Internet addresses are provided.

Bridge

Since February 1998 Bridge have been issuing a monthly newsletter that addresses how they are dealing with specific issues and follows through with deadlines and timetables.

Their approach has been to work with customers within a taskforce framework, to ensure that user requirements are fully met. They state that they will not remove any of their products as a result of the introduction of the Euro. Furthermore, they state in their newsletter that 'Bridge's Foreign Exchange database is prepared for the Euro and we are prepared to accept securities denominated in the new currency. In addition, Bridge is able to accept "backfills" of synthetic history from exchanges and OTC contributors when data is available.'

In summary, their approach to the main issues include the following.

Historical conversions

They are addressing three main areas: raw data cut, redenomination and synthetic histories.

Dual instruments

They plan to make dual reporting available.

Test data

They are working towards providing testing during the third and fourth quarters. A timetable will be published in due course.

Cost

There will not be any additional costs for the provision of their service due to changes made as a result of the introduction of the Euro.

More information can be found on their Website: www.bridge.com, under 'Customer Service'.

Bloomberg

Bloomberg are taking a pro-active stance in respect of the introduction of the Euro. The following information has been gained from the Bloomberg Euro information service. (See Bloomberg, Euro <go>.)

Equity

It was thought that, to ensure the continuity of prices, there need only be one-off adjustments to their histories using the relevant accession rates. The introduction of the Euro could be viewed in a similar manner to seismic changes in circumstances such as tax or budget provisions, government legislation, and so on, and so should have little effect on the validity of past data in the context of technical analysis.

Debt

It was suggested that, in any participating currency, the default risk for corporate bonds should not change, but that there might be a change in the default risk of government bonds. It was pointed out that, to some extent, there is already a risk of default on the government bonds of any country whose central bank is truly independent. In any case, the effects on prices should be a gradual adjustment rather than a one-off quantum change on accession day. The repercussions of default risk would be seen in the areas of analysis: for example, the choice of a risk-free rate in derivative valuation and the selection of a default-free zero-coupon yield curve.

Currencies

Several suggestions are made as to how to analyse the volatility of the Euro prior to accession day and how to create a synthetic history for the Euro.

Questions and answers

Bloomberg also provide a number of questions with answers that address specific impacts on their systems.

Share prices for 'in' countries will be backdated using the fixed exchange rate for the underlying currency. How will Bloomberg backdate share prices?

For 'out' countries, assuming that the local quote is maintained, any new quote in Euros will be treated as any other new secondary quote and no back history will be generated. Conversely, assuming that the local quote is scrapped, back history will be generated using the selected method chosen by the client, in the Personal Default Setting, PDS.

What currency choices will be available for cross-currency analysis?

The required choice will depend on the user and the stock, e.g. French investors will want to make currency translation into the Euro based on the French franc and the fixed conversion factor, whereas the UK investor may wish to see a UK company translated into the Euro based on a weighted basket basis.

Bloomberg will meet these varied needs by offering several choices that the user can select in PDF. In addition, there will be currency tickers for the Euro backdating history from each participating currency.

Will stock keep its old Bloomberg mnemonic/ISIN code/SEDOL?

For 'in' countries it is likely that Euro pricing will replace local pricing on 4th January 1999, in which case the old Bloomberg mnemonics will be used for the quote in Euros. They are waiting for the clarification of the approach to ISIN and SEDOLs by the various European exchanges.

If an 'in' exchange allows a local and Euro quote, then an additional Bloomberg mnemonic will be generated.

If a quote is a secondary quote in an 'out' country (in addition to the local currency), Bloomberg will treat it as any other secondary quote with an additional mnemonic. It is still to be decided what they will do if the quote replaces the local currency.

Will redenomination of the share capital affect the analysis?

Redenomination of the share capital itself will have minimal impact on analysis or Bloomberg's screens. However, some companies may take the opportunity to adjust the number of shares in issue. This will have an impact, but should be treated as any other share split/consolidation.

How will Bloomberg display accounting data information before/after the Euro?

Over the three year transition period companies will switch to accounting in Euros. Therefore, Bloomberg will allow the user the choice of whether to view the historic and current accounting information in Euros or the local currency. This will allow comparisons on a consistent basis. RV, FA and ESRC will also have a flag to ensure consistent comparisons across companies.

How will Bloomberg adjust historic accounts?

Bloomberg will follow the FEE recommendations and adjust accounts on a fixed exchange rate basis.

Different countries will account for the Euro costs differently, so how will this affect the cross-currency comparisons between companies?

Bloomberg employ a team of 150 people who adjust companies' accounts to ensure that they can be seen on a consistent basis.

How will dividends in Euros affect the analysis?

Dividends could be paid in local currency or the Euro. Bloomberg will recognise the currency of the dividend and the share and make the relevant adjustments.

How will convertibles be treated?

It is likely that the convertible will be:

a) quoted by units, e.g. 40 Euros per nominal (the functions will be adjusted to ensure the yield and other characteristics are unchanged)
b) the bond may eventually be redenominated leading to a change in terms (Bloomberg will ensure the relevant data terms are adjusted), or
c) during the transition period the convertible will be quoted in local currency and settled in the Euro (analytical functions need not change; however, invoicing functions will offer a choice of local or Euro currency, automatically doing the translation).

This is unless the convertible already contains special terms.

Historic volatility for shares

As the share prices are adjusted back in time by fixed exchange rates, there will be no jump or sudden change of historic volatility due to the treatment of the prices.

Volatility measures the proportional change or speed of the share, not the absolute change or speed. Changing the value on a consistent fixed basis does not affect the proportional change and therefore there will be no impact on historic volatility.

Financial Times Information

Financial Times Information (FTI) present the following information in their focal point bulletin and their paper, *European Monetary Union – The Impact on Financial Times Information's Market Data Services*:

- Irrevocable exchange rates will be supplied on '1' series SEDOL numbers for Exshare, FTS and SVS and in Exshare F4 Header Records.
- FTI will show prices as reported by individual exchanges. Since the European exchanges are considering a big bang approach this means reporting in the Euro for member states from 4th January 1999.
- Where a security is priced in a dual quote, FTI products will carry Euro prices only.
- A new setting of an existing Exshare/FTS data item will be used to show where a security has changed its pricing currency to the Euro, but where the currency of the nominal has not changed.
- Changes in ISIN and SEDOL will be incorporated if and when they take place. Currently (February 1998) full details of changes are not available, although it is understood that France and Holland have decided to make changes to ISIN numbers whilst others are

undecided. SEDOL numbers are not likely to change as a result of redenomination.

- Cash paybacks and the consideration of fractions will depend on which method companies use to redenominate. FTI will aim to show this data within existing income data fields, as is done for other types of capital repayment. New markers to identify that the capital repayment relates to a security's redenomination will be allocated as required.

- Redenomination of a security will take place as information is released. At present, it is expected that European governments' debt will be redenominated on 4th January 1999, other bonds may not change until later and equities may move to no par value.

- Income amounts will always be shown as announced by the company concerned, whether they are national legacy or Euro. Where a company announces both, the main income announcement will be shown in Euros with the national legacy currency being shown with a setting of 86 in the income sub-section code.

- If governments do redenominate debt FTI may supply a special 'set-up' service or formatted report. In reality, most governments are likely to redenominate their debt.

- All actual dividends will be shown as announced. FTI supply forecast information and annualised figures; changes within these forecasts will be decided upon with input from clients.

- Capital events will be shown as announced, with no conversion of currency amounts. If they are announced in dual currencies, FTI will use the Euro.

- FTI will introduce changes before the conversion weekend to help smooth out the volume of information being passed through their systems over the conversion weekend.

- WM/Reuters intend to supply a spot closing service of rates against the Euro from 4th January 1999. These will be included within FTI services.

- FTI are currently reviewing the effects on indices.

Further information can be obtained from FTI's Website www.fti.com or from their Focal Point Bulletin. To discuss specific issues, Financial Times Information's Customer Support Team should be consulted.

ICV/Datastream

ICV/Datastream have stated that they will be ready for the introduction of the Euro on 4th January 1999, when 'the European Exchanges implement a "big bang" for the introduction of the Euro'. In particular they state:

- Existing codes for equities from all EMU countries will switch to Euro quotes from the first day of business.
- All history for these stocks will be converted to Euros by Datastream prior to the start of business. Histories will be converted using the fixed conversion rates.
- Datastream have a business continuance plan in place to cope with the eventuality that one country drops out of EMU or EMU collapses completely. They will retain national currency historical data and the routines to convert security codes would be reversed to appropriate national currencies.
- Sterling or other joining countries could be incorporated into the system automatically.
- There are no additional costs for generic changes to the system. If an organisation requires advice on macros and system configuration then this may be chargeable.
- Tools will be available to allow conversion via any of the EMU currencies, via the Euro, via fixed conversion rates or via synthetic rates.
- Different views will be available for data through functions such as 'tilde'.
- If an issue is allocated a new ISIN code then they will store the existing ISIN code in a new field and update the ISIN field with the new code. The security will be stored under the same Datastream code.
- If organisations report in national currencies, Datastream will automatically convert this data and provide both national currency and Euro views.
- If an issuer redenominates an issue then so will Datastream.

For further information, their Website can provide further data: www.primark.com.

Reuters

Reuters have published information regarding their Euro programme on the Internet and on their real-time IDN data network. To see the latest update of this information, you can view their Website: www.reuters.com or access their real-time system by viewing page EURO. Their approach to the Euro can be summarised as follows.

Capacity and performance

Reuters believe that the introduction of the Euro will not give rise to any changes in data volumes or update rates in the markets. However, they believe that it will lead to an increase in the number of Reuters' Instrument Codes (RICs), although this will be well within the spare capacity of their system.

Dual reporting

It is not the intention of Reuters to provide dual quotes, since they believe that it will cause unnecessary cost and capacity burdens on communication links and caches in clients' systems. They believe that by using the locking rates data it will possible for many applications and presentations to show quotations both in the Euro and national legacy currencies.

Reuters plan to continue to use national legacy currency quotes and rates beyond 1st January 1999 as well as the Euro.

They will not be using the Euro symbol, but will instead be using the 'EUR' currency code.

Synthetic history

Reuters plan to offer a synthetic history per participating currency re-based to the historic performance of the legacy currency. They also plan to provide a synthetic history based on the history of the ECU.

In addition, they are planning to provide historic GDP data by country that will allow customers to carry out price history modelling with their own software.

Equity markets

Reuters expect countries both within EMU and outside of EMU to quote equity prices in the Euro from 4th January 1999. They have suggested that since no single market convention has been developed on how to convert historic data for stocks or shares they are currently planning a flat rate conversion using the irrevocable fixing rates announced on 31st December 1998. Customers of Reuters will be able to use a number of synthetic histories as outlined above.

Test data

It is Reuters' intention to make demonstration data available over their network to allow their customers to have a prior view of how data may change. The first types of data that are likely to be available are records relating to the new currency itself. Reuters state that this data will be static and should not be used by customers as the basis for comprehensive pre-Euro simulations in complex situations. Rather, customers should use the data in key example testing. They suggest that this data will be available on their live network, rather than a separate testbed.

5 Managing the introduction of the Euro

The introduction of the Euro is an event the likes of which has never been seen before. However, managing its introduction should be like any other project or group of projects. As seen in the previous chapters, the introduction of the Euro will affect many operational areas: front office, back office, accounts, supporting technologies and information sources. To this extent, any Euro-related changes should be regarded as a programme of work and should follow a standard project life cycle.

There are many approaches that are variations on the same theme. The approach described in this chapter is based on experience. It can be summarised as:

- initiation
- analysis
- design and development
- testing
- implementation.

Initiation

Before a programme can commence it is important to gain approval for the project and lay out the initial scope of the work to be undertaken. It is important to think through the reason for the programme, its objectives and what it will achieve at a strategic level. To help in this process, a number of tools can be used: the mission statement and setting down the objectives.

Mission statement

The first thing that needs to be established is the reason for a project, its *raison d'être*. The mission statement has become a trendy concept in recent years, but it has its value in focusing the programme. The mission statement might be as simple as:

'The aim of any Euro programme is to ensure that our organisation can operate normally in the Euro from 4th January 1999.'

Objectives

Once the primary focus has been defined, it is important to interpret it and scope out the main objectives. These might look like this:

1. To ensure that we are Euro compliant prior to the start of wholesale market operations in the Euro on Monday 4th January 1999. This means:
    *   the programme will work to ensure that business systems are ready for the Euro
    *   the programme will work to ensure that supporting IT systems are ready
    *   the programme will work to ensure that system changes have been made to encompass changes to information feeds.
2. To ensure that we are ready for a company-wide test of our capability to operate when the Euro is launched before the beginning of December 1998.
3. To ensure that we have the ability to participate in any market-wide testing that may take place in the fourth quarter of 1998.

Strategic approach

Delivering these specific Euro-related objectives requires the implementation of several phases, from a thorough investigation of the problem through to testing and implementation prior to and over the conversion weekend. These stages can be summarised as:

- business impact analysis
- design and development
- testing
- implementation (including the conversion weekend).

Ultimately, the timing of a Euro programme is determined by the introduction of the Euro on 1st January 1999. This is a date that cannot be moved and any programme cannot afford to slip; business and IT systems must be ready to go live over the conversion weekend. This means that analysis, design and development and testing must be completed before this date.

In addition, any market-wide testing will take place towards the end of 1998. Organisations wishing to be involved in such tests must have some, or all, of their business and IT systems in place before then. However, this does not mean that an organisation should, or necessarily has to, participate in a company-wide test at this time. It may be that some business areas, such as custodian links and database processes, and so on could be tested separately. It would therefore be advantageous if solutions have been implemented as early as possible, but not essential.

At this early stage, the remaining areas should be planned out at a strategic level; this might look something like this:

	April	May	June	July	Aug	Sept	Oct	Nov	Dec
Impact Assessment	▓	▓							
Design and Development		▓	▓	▓	▓	▓			
Testing				▓	▓	▓	▓	▓	
Implementation							▓	▓	▓

The table shows that not every area needs to be completed before another can commence. The limited time that is available to complete this work means that, where possible, the next stage should start at the earliest opportunity. For example, once the impacts on a computer system become known, then someone can start to work on the solution before other areas are completed. Each of these areas can now be taken in turn and broken down further.

Business impact analysis

Before any changes can be made the full impact of the introduction of the Euro must be assessed. Hopefully, this guide can provide you with many of the answers and highlight many of the impacts your organisation faces. However, because the introduction of the Euro is a one-off event and completely new, no one knows all of the answers and many issues and impacts are emerging daily.

To assess the impacts on a particular organisation, further analysis and research must be undertaken. There are many sources of information that can provide guidance and answers to the many unresolved questions. The information source in the last chapter of this book will be of considerable help.

Structuring the investigation will be one of the keys to its success. Like any project, the analysis must follow a structure and be well managed if it is to succeed within the timescales enforced upon it. In the previous chapters the impacts have been broken down into separate areas: by business area, IT and information service providers. This structure can help focus investigations, although the business areas can be broken down still further to strategic impacts and operational ones.

Organisations must focus on the impacts on their ability to operate a normal level of service come January 1999. They must address each of the areas and find their own solutions. Examples of investigations in each area follow.

Business strategy

The introduction of the Euro is a business issue with wide-ranging impacts. The structure of the European wholesale money markets is set to change overnight and this means that the environment in which a financial organisation operates will change and consequently so will the rules and boundaries that previously governed it. It is therefore important that these changes are considered at an early stage, since they will have an effect on business operations and supporting systems. The types of questions to be considered include:

- What will be the impact of the move towards a sector, rather than country, basis?
- Do we want to invest more in the European equity market?
- Should we, ethically, invest more in Europe? Can we? What do our trustees or clients want?
- As a company, should we issue our own debt on a Euro basis?
- Should we consider reassessing our investment approach in other markets?
- Will we be over-exposed to the Euro market?
- Do we want to receive payments only in the Euro?

Business operations

Business operations can be said to be the day-to-day operations of an organisation. As such, it is important that they are addressed by ground-level, operational staff, people who are going to be affected by change on a daily basis. Analysis should involve partnership between a business analyst assigned to co-ordinate the investigation of the impacts and specific personnel. Questions include:

- How will the treasury department reconcile our position for the 11 countries over the conversion weekend?
- Can our custodians cope with the introduction of the Euro? What are they doing to prepare for it?
- Can we cope with the introduction of the Euro in deal entry?
- What are our brokers doing?
- Will there be any changes to our reporting requirements?
- What are our counterparties' intentions?
- Can we form one nostro account for our Euro business?

Information technology

Today, information technology supports a wide range of business activities. It helps to streamline business operations and allows a further level of control to be applied. To ensure that it continues to satisfy these requirements after the introduction of the Euro in January 1999 many changes will need to be made. Understanding these problems requires that many areas are addressed. This should not be done in isolation, but with an understanding of the impacts on business operations. Some of the key questions include:

- What is the impact of the introduction of the Euro on our spreadsheets?
- Can our main database cope with the additional currency?
- How do we cope with historical data on the system?
- Do our systems have the ability to take two decimal places?
- Will users require screens to change?
- Will the users require changes to be made to reports?
- Do our systems calculate to six decimal places?
- Can we have dual quotes or just one?
- Can our systems cope with the changes that are going to be made by Reuters, Bloomberg, and so on?

It is important that a full impact assessment on IT systems is carried out as soon as is possible because the impacts are likely to be substantial and finding resources and actually undertaking development and testing work will require much time and effort. The impacts need to be formally documented in order that later stages can be carried out successfully.

Information services

The majority of financial organisations are reliant on information – information relating to prices, historical performance, stock availability, new issues, dividends, and so on. Understanding the changes in information provided and making adequate preparation should be a key objective. Some of the questions that should be asked include:

- How are Reuters going to supply stock price information? Are they going to quote dual prices?
- Will they supply accurate historical data?
- Will they charge for any changes?
- Will their screens change?

Documenting the impacts

As the impacts become known they should be documented and recommendations for developing solutions should be put forward to the appropriate senior management. The infrastructure of a programme is discussed later. This document should be a full impact assessment of the whole of the business, split into the relevant sections.

One way of focusing attention on the information is to document the issues and risks that an organisation faces and the assumptions that can be made. Issues can be viewed as areas where an impact will occur: for example, the introduction of the Euro will have an impact on Eurozone nostro accounts, dividends will be received in Euros and Eurozone equities will be priced in Euros. Risks include the fact that the breakup of EMU will have an impact on any system changes that have been made. Assumptions, on the other hand, are things that can be taken for granted either because they are part of legislation, they are part of market practice or because they are things that have been decided upon by an organisation at a strategic level; for example, the conversion of 'in' currencies must be to six significant figures, the wholesale market operations will be carried out primarily in the Euro: WWFM will operate in Euros and not in the national currencies from 4th January 1999.

The benefits of documenting these areas in this way is that it can form the basis for carrying out the next stage and can be communicated to relevant parties quickly and effectively.

Design and development

This stage of the project is concerned with designing solutions to meet the impacts identified in the previous stage. If issues and risks have been generated then it is important to categorise them by area of impact and the level of impact itself. For example:

ID	Risk or Issue Level	Area	Issue or Risk	Task	Responsi-bility
1	High	Strategic	There is likely to be a draw towards the Eurozone equity market as a result of the convergence of the market.	Carry out further analysis of the impacts of this on the European and UK portfolio and draft a set of recommendations for senior management.	Senior economist

2	High	Ops	Will it be more desirable to have a pan-Eurozone index rather than separate ones?	Fund managers to assess the need for a pan-European index and put forward proposal.	European fund manager
3	Medium	IT	Key boards must have the ability to have the Euro symbol placed within them as soon as possible.	The IT/procurement manager needs to ensure that this requirement is held in mind when purchasing new hardware.	IT/ procurement manager
4	High	Strategic	Some UK equity may be redenominated into the Euro. Do we want to be able to buy and sell Euro-denominated UK stocks?	Further investigation of the impacts and the drafting of recommendations for senior management and subsequently clients and trustees.	Fund managers
5	Low	Strategic	When the UK adopts the Euro it will have an impact on the UK portfolio.	In the long-run a review of the impacts is required and a strategic plan for moving to the position of the UK being in EMU.	UK fund manager
6	High	Ops	The conversion of standing data relating to the 11 currencies entering EMU will need to be changed prior to 4th January 1999.	Review the situation at a detailed level and develop alternatives for managing the impact.	IT business analyst standing data manager

Breaking down the impacts in this way and assigning someone responsibility will aid in their resolution.

Sometimes designing and developing a solution will require original thought, whilst at other times there will be a need to follow legislative or market-driven assumptions. As mentioned above, it is important to understand these assumptions as they will provide many of the answers. It is helpful to break them down into legal and market-driven.

Assumptions driven by legislation

- A system must be able to calculate foreign exchanges to six significant figures.
- Exchange rates will be quoted with the Euro as the primary currency, i.e. £0.7 to one Euro.
- Nominal values of bonds will have to be held to two decimal places.
- A system must be able to input an exchange rate to six decimal places.
- Conversion of currencies must only be by division, multiplying the inverse is not acceptable.
- A system must be able to use the ISO standard 'EUR' symbol for the Euro.

Assumptions driven by market practice

- Custodians will open Euro accounts for each portfolio in the last quarter of 1998.
- Dividends and coupons for 'in' countries will become payable to clients in Euros, irrespective of what currency they were paid in.
- A reconciliation will take place pre- and post-conversion weekend.
- Reconvention of bonds will be via a corporate action.

Providing business solutions

Since the introduction of the Euro is primarily a business issue it will have a huge effect on business strategy and business processes. Care should be taken to ensure that action is being made towards resolving the impacts identified in an impact assessment. There will be one person within an organisation who has a grounded understanding of a particular area of operation and it should be their responsibility to assess issues and provide recommendations for their resolution.

Ultimately, the Euro programme manager will have responsibility for ensuring that people are carrying out the required work.

Education and information

The introduction of the Euro will affect many areas of an organisation's business operations and supporting systems. As a result many people within organisations will be directly affected and their help will be required in carrying out the programme. They may be required for helping to find solutions or for user testing. In addition, many other people will also be indirectly affected and it is important that the programme and the impacts of the introduction of the Euro are communicated to them. There is therefore an ongoing need to communicate both the issues relating to EMU and the progress of the Euro programme itself to an organisation's personnel.

Information may be relayed in the form of meetings, a newsletter or the intranet. A Euro programme team may even have a library set up where people can come and either use the information for their own impact assessment or look up more general concerns.

Keeping an eye on longer-term issues

It is also important during the design and development stage that the longer-term issues are borne in mind. Specifically, issues that will affect operations when the UK joins EMU must be logged in order that progress can be made towards their resolution after the conversion weekend. These will cover all of the other areas previously considered for the start of the Eurozone in January 1999, particularly the impacts on IT systems, the changes in business strategy and the business processes.

Providing IT solutions

Providing solutions to the impacts on IT systems is key to being ready for the introduction of the Euro in January 1999. Current systems and new systems alike, such as Cash Position applications, need to be changed during 1998.

The impact report (see p. 65) completed as part of the impact assessment should be used as the basis for this work. It is important that design and development is undertaken in a formal and documented manner that reflects the normal practices of an organisation. If work is to be carried out by vendors or an outsourcing company then an organisation must obtain guarantees that the work will be completed in the timescales set out previously. If these external suppliers do not deliver then there may be serious consequences.

Obtaining skilled staff is also going to be a problem for many organisations. It may be that there are no in-house staff that can undertake the changes, because they are working on Y2K projects for example, or because there are other projects being undertaken that cannot stop. It may also be the case that the impacts are so vast that many additional people are required. The impacts are not necessarily complicated, they will merely require a high number of man-hours to fix. If an organisation faces such circumstances then it must turn to the market for contract workers. However, managers must be prepared to pay a premium for staff, since demand for people with relevant knowledge and experience is high because of the imminent introduction of the Euro and the approaching Millennium.

Testing

The introduction of the Euro will affect business systems and supporting IT systems from 1st January 1999. Once changes have been made to these systems they must be fully tested in order to ensure that they will work when they are delivered to a live environment. Fundamentally, testing should follow an organisation's general testing strategy and should address not only IT systems but also business systems. Due to the imposed timescales this work should begin no later than the end of June 1998 and be completed by the end of November.

To co-ordinate testing and allow for the more advanced areas to be tested first, sections of the business and IT should be broken down into separate areas. They can then be tested as units.

Once many units have been tested it will be necessary to undertake a system test to ensure that they continue to work when they are linked together again. It may also be necessary to undertake a company-wide Euro test before the end of November 1998. This date would allow for system developments to be implemented and problems put right before the conversion weekend. This might be combined with a Millennium test.

Any new systems that are currently being implemented must also be investigated and tested for Euro compliance. Do they meet the changed specifications? Do the interfaces still operate on the same basis?

It is generally agreed that there will be a market-wide test for Euro compliance at the end of the third quarter and beginning of the fourth quarter of 1998. Organisations may wish to be involved in such testing, and therefore should plan to be ready to do so.

Implementation

Implementation is about making changes to the live environment. Both business and IT changes will take on various formats over the lifetime of EMU.

Implementation prior to the conversion weekend

Initially, there will be an opportunity for some changes to be implemented prior to the conversion weekend. It will be possible to add the 'EUR' currency code to systems, add Euro terms and conditions to derivative contracts, set up standing data tables, set up a Euro nostro account, agree strategic options for the business, and so on. As suggested before, these changes should be thoroughly tested before they are imported into a live environment and change controls should be applied at all times.

However, many of these activities will be limited because the conversion rates of 'in' currencies will not be fixed until 1st January 1999. This will require changes to be made over the conversion weekend.

The conversion weekend

The conversion weekend will commence at the end of play on 30th December 1998 for some institutions, the 31st for others, and finish on 4th January 1999 for all. The main changes that will have to be introduced over the weekend include:

- the redenomination of outstanding debt issues of governments and other issuers into the Euro
- the conversion of 11 'in' cash accounts into the Euro
- the conversion of prices from 11 national currencies into the Euro
- the redenomination of some equity holdings from national legacy currencies into the Euro
- the implementation of supporting systems to the live environment
- supporting IT systems in the live environment
- the implementation of business continuance plans.

Planning these activities will be an in-depth process. Whilst many of the tasks will be specific to organisations, many of the tasks required to be undertaken will be generic and can be summarised as:

- Custodians should have informed organisations which issues are going to be redenominated, although they will not be able to be physically converted until the official rates are agreed on 1st January 1999. Details of when this information will be available and how it will be communicated to organisations must be clarified as soon as possible. This will be a process that will continue for much of the third quarter of 1998. A final list of the securities that will be redenominated should be published no later than 30th September 1998.
- There should be a reconciliation before and after the conversion weekend from the custodians. This will ensure that any discrepancies caused by the introduction of the Euro are identified and dealt with. Reconciliation of Euro impacts will be much harder if this is left to a later date.
- All new securities issued during the last quarter of 1998 should be accompanied by detailed information relating to their redenomination into a Euro format.
- Existing holdings must be reconciled. The Bank of England has stated that it believes fund managers should not wait for advice from Central Securities Depositories (CSDs) or International CSDs (ICSDs) and custodians. Rather, they should redenominate and convert their positions, open trades and accounts as soon as possible over the conversion weekend, as a normal end of year process. Then they should reconcile this with information received from the custodians and securities depositories after the introduction of the Euro and changes have been implemented.
- The redenomination process will inevitably lead to rounding differences. It is important that organisations obtain clear information from their custodians on how adjustments will be made to their accounts. It is the responsibility of the individual organisation to check that their custodian has made adequate preparations for the conversion weekend.
- Standard settlement instructions for securities transactions must be changed to reflect changes due to the introduction of the Euro. These instructions should be communicated to counterparties before the final quarter of 1998.
- Various messaging systems will be used over the weekend by market participants to convey information about the redenomination process and the results. SWIFT will be an integral player in this process and they have provided guidance that should be used within the plans for the conversion weekend.

Post-conversion weekend

After the conversion weekend there will be a need to continue with the design, development and implementation of changes to current work systems. The main work will revolve around the entry of the UK into EMU, thought to be around 2002. The impacts will be much greater than those experienced now because accounting systems will need to be changed, strategic impacts on equity and debt markets will be on the home market and the domestic banking sector will also change.

However, the issues related to this period are not just focused on the UK joining. For the next three years European organisations will redenominate their capital share value and debt issues. There will be daily redenominations and renominalisations and these will need to be managed on an active basis. Organisations must consider how they are going to do this. Since this information will be communicated via corporate actions they have to consider whether they will take these actions daily or weekly in batch format. Will they receive them by email, the Internet, disk, manually, custodian links, or SWIFT 500 category messages? These actions must form a normal part of back office operations for the next three years.

However, it is likely that if EMU is seen as a success there will be other members wanting to join. The UK and Sweden in particular are likely to join and there will be mini conversion weekends throughout the next few years. These, in turn, will have transitional periods of around three years where organisations can redenominate. There is then the longer-term situation that will arise; other countries will join the European Union and, consequently, EMU. This will be especially true if the Euro begins to compete with the dollar as a reserve currency. These countries will also have conversion periods that will need to be managed. In summary, the introduction of the Euro is not a one-off event, in the sense that it will be a continual operation for the next decade or so. Managing this should be one of the considerations of any programme.

Business continuance

Business continuance must be considered as part of the overall strategy. It is important that throughout the project, change management procedures are stringently applied and that strategies and plans are put in place to handle the possibility that one or more countries drop out of EMU or EMU as a whole collapses. The risks and recommendations for managing them can be summarised as follows.

Risks

- If any one country drops out of EMU then any changes made to business and IT systems will be impacted post-implementation. This will cause a minor impact on normal operations.
- The potential collapse of EMU as a whole poses a most serious threat to normal business operations.

Recommendations

A business continuance strategy, with detailed plans and documentation, should be developed during the design and development stage to allow for the removal of one or more countries from EMU or its complete collapse.

Should any one country drop out of EMU then that country must form a new currency, since the old national legacy currency is a denomination of the Euro. The currency must not take the form of any currency gone before it or be called the same as a previous currency. The result would be that a country dropping out would be more than likely to create something along the lines of a New French Franc (NF?). In such a case, Euro-denominated stock would have to be redenominated into the new currency; so too would any old national currency stock. It would be a messy exercise, but can easily be managed if considered as a new currency within existing systems. However, planning for this event, even if it is only at a strategic level, will help to manage the risk.

If the whole of EMU collapses then this exercise must be repeated 11 times. It is therefore worth thinking through the implications of such an exercise and putting a strategy in place to deal with it, however unlikely it may seem.

Risk

The potential collapse of one or more external systems over the conversion weekend, such as any of the settlement systems, would have serious implications for the ability of an organisation to carry out normal business operations.

Recommendation

Contingency plans should be developed by a disaster recovery officer, in partnership with operational staff, to ensure that a company can continue to operate in the event of an external system failure. These plans should be supported by the appropriate documentation. This may be as simple as finding out about the different information service providers or settlement methods or settlement vehicles. Whilst it is unlikely that any of the main systems will fail to operate it is a possibility, even if it is caused by overload.

6   Programme infrastructure

The management of a Euro programme will require careful planning and control if it is to be delivered within the timescales imposed by the introduction of the Euro on 1st January 1999. At a strategic level, in order to achieve this, a programme must be embarked upon that is structured and provides a high level of control. This section outlines the resource requirement for the programme infrastructure.

Detailed planning

A strategic plan will need to be mapped out in detail. This should cover all aspects of the programme, including user input requirements as well as infrastructure work, such as project meetings and progress reporting. The areas to be planned in detail include:

- design and development of business solutions
- design and development of IT solutions
- detailed impact assessment of IT systems
- testing existing IT system
- implementation of business solutions
- implementation of IT solutions
- the conversion weekend

- project management activities.

It is also important that any current projects are impacted upon as little as possible by the work on the Euro and this should be an integral part of the Euro programme planning. Planning will need to be undertaken in partnership with the current planning requirements. Specifically, this means, where necessary:

- co-ordinating the planning of infrastructure work
- co-ordinating the planning of new projects (including the Y2K).

Roles and responsibilities

The key resources in a project aimed at ensuring Euro readiness can be summarised as:

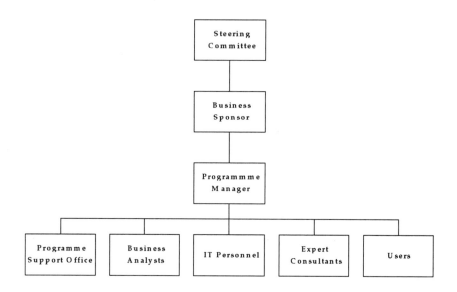

All of the resources will play a vital role in ensuring the successful delivery of the Euro programme. The roles and responsibilities of the main players can be further expanded.

Steering committee

Fundamentally, the introduction of the Euro is a business issue that needs to be managed by an organisation. As presented in Chapter 1, the general approach is to set up a steering committee to guide the project and ensure that progress is being made. In summary, the steering committee is ultimately responsible for the following:

- approving key business decisions
- approving the plan for design and development, testing, implementation and the conversion weekend
- checking project progress
- taking major decisions on the scope and direction of the project as they become apparent
- setting priorities for the project
- signing-off end of stage reports/documents.

Business sponsor

The business sponsor should be a key person from the business who is also on the steering committee. They are responsible for ensuring the requirements and scope of the programme are properly defined and the benefits realised. Their responsibilities can be summarised as:

- delivering the benefits of the programme
- providing momentum to the programme
- communicating the objectives, scope and benefits of the programme in terms of business and IT systems
- identifying the right users
- ensuring the functional specification of changes are accurate and signed-off (specific area representatives will be responsible for their respective areas)
- ensuring that users receive training
- ensuring that the steering committee are kept up to date with changes in costs and benefits
- always involving the programme manager in managing risks and issues
- controlling the scope of the programme.

Programme manager

Keeping the programme on target will require a senior programme manager with appropriate experience in running major projects. The nature of EMU means that it will cover many aspects of an organisation's operations. The person running the day-to-day management of the programme must be able to co-ordinate all areas and must have the personal ability to deal with all levels of management. The programme manager should be responsible for the following:

- supporting the programme sponsor in managing the business case
- identifying and managing risks and issues within the programme
- managing the programme on a daily basis – ensuring progress is being made
- delivering programme deliverables of each stage on time
- considering the relevant people, skill and job completion for components of the programme
- implementing a quality control process and ensuring that the programme deliverables meet the required standards
- managing the expectations of the users
- managing IT aspects of the Euro programme at a strategic level
- managing the business analysts
- liaising with expert consultants.

Programme support office

Any programme will require careful management and control if it is to be delivered within the timescales imposed by the introduction of the Euro. In order to achieve this, a programme support office should be put in place to monitor progress, co-ordinate business and IT issues and plan forthcoming work. In summary, their role can be said to be:

- detailed planning
- arranging weekly meetings
- checking progress of all involved in the programme
- managing the expectations of users
- reporting progress to the programme manager
- monitoring issues and risks
- distributing documentation
- ensuring that change control procedures are adhered to in all instances of code and business change
- liaising withand managing external contacts.

The number of people needed to provide this support will depend on the size of the organisation, the work being undertaken and the nature of the issues and changes that are being implemented.

Business analysts

There is a need to continually assess the business impact of the introduction of the Euro and ensure that business solutions are successfully implemented. Therefore, any programme should employ the services of business analysts to investigate the implications within these areas and ensure that business solutions are realised. The number of analysts required by an organisation will depend on the size of the organisation and the nature of their business. The more products and services they have in the European market place the more business analysts they will require. The main responsibilities of a business analyst will include:

- analysis of the implications of the introduction of EMU on business and IT systems
- documenting the findings of literature reviews
- documenting the findings of workshops and focus groups
- providing users with a resource to investigate specific implications within their areas
- writing reports
- modelling the impacts on the key areas
- co-ordinating all business issues – ensuring that there are no overlaps, or things missed
- ensuring that business solutions are delivered
- working with the IT analysts to ensure that systems are developed to reflect the requirements of EMU
- working with procurement to ensure that new products are compliant and to give advice when developing business/IT criteria.

IT personnel

Although the introduction of the Euro is a business issue it will require many changes to IT and information systems. As a result, IT people will be required throughout the life cycle of any Euro programme. Analyst programmers, testers and developers will be needed to make changes to current systems to enable the use of the Euro, the conversion of currencies, the redenomination of securities, the introduction of nominal decimal places, and so on.

Expert consultants

Throughout the life cycle of a project there will be a need for input from people who can provide expert knowledge and advice to the programme team and steering committee. Such personnel should provide information and skills in the areas of:

- the impacts on business strategy
- the impacts on business operations
- the impacts on IT systems
- the impacts on information systems.

Users

Many of the issues that the introduction of the Euro will bring will be focused at an operational level. Therefore, users will be required to provide input into any Euro programme. Many of the issues will be specific to the introduction of the Euro in January 1999 and will involve the following responsibilities:

- investigating the impact of the Euro within their own areas
- identifying and providing the business analysts with information reflecting business practices
- taking part in focus groups and discussion forums
- defining user and manual procedures (working practices) – if not already available
- testing any changes in business practices or IT applications
- testing any changes made to IT systems
- signing-off changes.

Each area should have a co-ordinator, usually the departmental manager, who is responsible for ensuring that their area is committed to the Euro project and undertakes appropriate actions. This person sits on the Euro steering committee and is required to sign-off requirements and design specifications for their specific area.

7 A guide to Euro compliance of new products

It is not my intention to suggest that the following is a fail-safe means of guaranting that a new product will be Euro compliant. However, it offers guidance on the drafting of a proposed Euro-compliant document. Any organisation intending to use such a document should seek the professional advice of a lawyer.

Products that use currency data must be checked for Euro compliance or Euro readiness. There are two basic degrees of Euro compliance:

Before UK entry

Whilst the UK remains outside of EMU the base currency of most organisations will remain in sterling. In respect of the 11 joining members, the Euro will replace national legacy currencies across the market.

After UK entry

If and when the UK joins EMU, organisations will move to replace sterling as their base currency with the Euro. This is assumed to be around 2002.

Criteria for Euro compliance

It is not enough for a supplier to state that it is Euro compliant. To be able to say that its product is compliant a vendor must be able to answer a number of criteria.

Before UK entry

- The system must be able to perform all its functions using the Euro currency as a replacement for the national legacy currencies of joining members.
- The system should be able to convert and round according to the requirements of the First Council Regulation.
- Any systems that interface with this system and use the Euro must be able to use appropriate file formats and values.
- The Euro symbol must be incorporated within screen layouts, reports, printing file formats and keyboard mappings.
- The system must round up where rounding takes place.

After UK entry

- The system must be able to continue to support business operations when the UK joins EMU. This means offering multiple currency functionality where appropriate, i.e. accounting systems, or direct transfer to using the Euro as a base currency with the ability to retrieve historical data containing sterling.

Future system enhancements

A product or service's failure to meet the criteria for compliance will not necessarily mean the product or service should be excluded from consideration. If an organisation can provide information proving that it will be compliant either before January 1999, in the case of the general requirements, or before the UK intends to join, 2002, it could be considered.

However, if a decision is taken to purchase a system based on the promise of a vendor to provide a Euro-compliant product then care must be taken to ensure that they are encouraged to stick to any plans to which they agree.

Warranty

Potential vendors must also be asked of their willingness to sign a warranty in the event that their product is chosen. Bird and Bird, the IT lawyers, suggest in a seminar paper, 'Understanding the legal implications of EMU', that a possible warranty might look something like this:

'The supplier warrants that the system is:

1. Capable of performing all functions set out in the specification for more than one currency and for the common currency of countries joining EMU, i.e. the Euro.
2. Compliant with all legal requirements applicable to the Euro in any jurisdiction, including, but without limitation, the rules on conversion and rounding set out in the EC Regulation number 1103/97.
3. Capable of displaying and printing, and will incorporate in all relevant layouts, all symbols and codes adopted by any government or any other European Union body in relation to the Euro.'

For further information see their website: www.twobirds.com

Responsibility for compliance

In the first place, it should be the responsibility of a project sponsor, with advice from the Euro programme team, to ensure that all aspects of Euro compliance have been considered. As a final check it should be the ultimate responsibility of the Chief Operations Officer to ensure that the product is Euro compliant before a purchase order can be raised.

Epilogue – a Euro future

As we enter the new Millennium, Europe and the world face huge changes. One main economic change will be the introduction of the Euro. Currently 11 currencies will be replaced by the Euro and these will be added to in the next few years. Sweden, Denmark and the UK are all set to join in the first few years of the next century. But what about Norway, Slovakia, Poland, Hungary, even Russia ? Will they seek to join the Dollar contender ?

The next decade will be the most challenging time for the new currency. It will be an infant with no history and no past, but it will have strong and determined parents – eleven in fact, who are some of the world's most powerful economic players.

Whatever economic arguments are used, the Euro is unlikely not to succeed. Many European politicians have made a single currency their life's work and so it is not likely that they will let it fail in their lifetime, whatever the cost. In addition, the cost of a failure, a break-up or a collapse, would be an economic world crisis, the like of which has never been seen before. Participating countries would have to buy back their Euro debt by issuing more debt in a new currency, recall overseas loans and tighten their domestic economies. It would virtually bankrupt them. For one country this would cause shock waves around the world, but for 11.....

Perhaps a more realistic scenario for the future is that by 2020 the Euro would be the common currency from Scandanavia in the north, the UK, France, Spain and Portugal in the west, Greece and Turkey in the south and the former Soviet Republics in the east. By then many nations would have rebalanced their foreign reserves and released billions of dollars onto the foreign exchange market, pushing the US into recession.

In response, the US government would approach the European Central Bank to discuss the possibility of setting up a new world currency: the Euro Dollar; in 2025 the first truly global currency is launched; by 2040 the last countries give up their national currencies and the Euro Dollar becomes the only legal currency of the world.

Whether or not this secenario comes true, we have to deal with the practicalities of the introduction of the Euro right now. Its introduction in January 1999 presents an unprecedented challenge to businesses. Understanding the impacts and actively managing them is the key to ensuring that business and technological solutions are delivered in time for the start. Whether you are for or against the Euro is not important. The Euro *will* be introduced on 1st January 1999 and to avoid business disadvantage you must investigate the impacts and implement changes to deal with them.

Hopefully, this book will have helped you to understand the main issues and given you a framework within which to work. Not every detail of stage 3 EMU is presented here: many of the finer details and market practices are emerging daily. However, further information is only a computer away via the internet and, where possible, I have tried to provide this information.

Acronyms

ANNA	Association of National Numbering Agencies
AGM	Annual General Meeting
BBA	British Bankers Association
CD	Certificate of Deposit
CGO	Central Gilts Office
CHAPS	Clearing House Automated Payment System
CMO	Central Money Markets Office
CSDs	Central Securities Depositories
EBA	ECU Banking Association
ECB	European Central Bank
ECOFIN	Economic and Finance Committee
EGM	Extraordinary General Meeting
EIB	European Investment Bank
EMI	European Monetary Institute
EMU	Economic and Monetary Union
EURIBOR	European Inter-bank Offer Rate
ESCB	European System of Central Banks
FEE	Federation des Experts Compatibles Europeens
FESE	Federation of European Stock Exchanges
FTSE	Financial Times Stock Exchanges (Indices)
ICSDs	International Central Securities Depositories
IFMA	Institutional Fund Managers' Association

IMRO	Investment Managers Regulatory Organisation
IPMA	International Primary Markets Association
ISDA	International Swaps and Derivatives Association
ISIN	International Securities Identification Number
ISO	International Standards Organisation
LIBA	London Investment Banking Association
LIBID	London Inter-Bank Bid Rate
LIBOR	London Inter-Bank Offer Rate
LIFFE	London International Financial Futures and Options Exchange
LSE	London Stock Exchange
LTD	Long Term Date
NCB	National Central Bank
NCU	National Currency Unit
OTC	Over the Counter
PDS	Personal Default Setting
PIBOR	Paris Inter-bank Offer Rate
RICs	Reuters' Instrument Codes
RTGS	Real-Time Gross Settlement System
SEDOL	Stock Exchange Daily Official List
STF	Spread Trading Facility
STIR	Short-Term Interest Rate
SWIFT	Society for Worldwide Interbank Financial Telecommunications
TARGET	Trans-European Automated Real-time Gross Settlement Express Transfer System
VPC	Voluntary Position Conversion
WWFM	World Wide Fund Managers

Sources of information

This section of the book is a reconciliation of all of the sources used in the development of this guide. However, as well as providing an audit of where the information has come from, it also gives the reader the opportunity to seek out further specific information.

Bank of England (August 1997) *Practical Issues Arising from the Introduction of the Euro No. 5*, London

Bank of England (December 1997) *Practical Issues Arising from the Introduction of the Euro No.6*, London

Bank of England (March 1998) *Practical Issues Arising from the Introduction of the Euro No. 7*, London

Bank of England website www.bankofengland.co.uk

Bird and Bird (November 1997) 'Understanding the legal implications of EMU', seminar paper

Bloomberg see Bloomberg system, Euro <go>

Bridge website www.bridge.com

The British Computer Society (September 1997) *Preparing for the Euro*, Wiltshire

Currie.,D. (1996, research report) 'The pros and cons of EMU', The Economist Intelligence Unit, London

Euroclear (September 1997, working document) *Opening the door to the Euro*; available on Euroclear website

Euroclear website: www.euroclear.com

European Commission (September 1997, draft exposure) 'Preparing information systems for the Euro', EU, Belgium; also available on EC website

European Commission website: www.europa.eu.int

Federation des Experts Comptables Europeans (FEE) website: www.euro.fee.be

Financial Times Information (FTI), Market Data Services: (1998, working paper) *European Monetary Union – The Impact on Financial Times Information's Market Data Services*, London

FTI website: www.fti.com

Hawkins, P. (1997) *A Concise Project Management Approach*

HM Treasury (July 1997) *EMU: Practical information for Business*; also available on HM Treasury website

The Hundred Group of Finance Directors (March 1997) *The Single European Currency*

ICV/Datastream website: www.primark.com

International Swaps and Derivatives Association (December 1997, memo) 'Operational issues for derivatives businesses'

Johnson., C. (1996) *In with the Euro out with the pound*, Penguin, London

LIFFE Market website: www.liffe.com

Microsoft website: premium.microsoft.com/support/office/content/tahoma/euro.asp

Reuters website: www.reuters.com

SWIFT website: euro@swift.com

UBS (December 1997) *Towards the Euro-zone, Threats and Opportunities for Companies and Investors*, UBS Global Research, London

Index